KU-154-009

Social Classes and Social Relations in Britain, 1850–1914

Prepared for
The Economic History Society by

ALASTAIR J. REID
Girton College,
Cambridge

POLYTECHNIC LIBRARY
WOLVERHAMPTON
802773
942.
081
REI
14. APR. 1992

M

© The Economic History Society 1992

All rights reserved. No reproduction, copy or transmission
of this publication may be made without written permission.

No paragraph of this publication may be reproduced, copied
or transmitted save with written permission or in accordance
with the provisions of the Copyright, Designs and Patents Act 1988
or under the terms of any licence permitting limited copying
issued by the Copyright Licensing Agency, 90, Tottenham Court Road,
London W1P 9HE.

Any person who does any unauthorised act in relation to
this publication may be liable to criminal prosecution and
civil claims for damages.

First published 1992

Published by
MACMILLAN EDUCATION LTD
Houndmills, Basingstoke, Hampshire RG21 2XS
and London
Companies and representatives
throughout the world

Typeset by Footnote Graphics,
Warminster, Wiltshire
Printed in Hong Kong

A catalogue record for this book
is available from the British Library.

ISBN 0–333–438469

Series Standing Order

If you would like to receive future titles in this series as they are
published, you can make use of our standing order facility. To place a
standing order please contact your bookseller or, in case of difficulty,
write to us at the address below with your name and address and the
name of the series. Please state with which title you wish to begin your
standing order. (If you live outside the United Kingdom we may not
have the rights for your area, in which case we will forward your order
to the publisher concerned.)

Customer Services Department, Macmillan Distribution Ltd
Houndmills, Basingstoke, Hampshire, RG21 2XS, England.

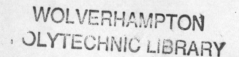
WOLVERHAMPTON
OLYTECHNIC LIBRARY

Contents

List of Tables

Editor's Preface

When this series was established in 1968 the first editor, the late Professor M. W. Flinn, laid down three guiding principles. The books should be concerned with important fields of economic history; they should be surveys of the current state of scholarship rather than a vehicle for the specialist views of the authors, and above all, they were to be introductions to their subject and not 'a set of pre-packaged conclusions'. These aims were admirably fulfilled by Professor Flinn and by his successor, Professor T. C. Smout, who took over the series in 1977. As it passes to its third editor and approaches its third decade, the principles remain the same.

Nevertheless, times change, even though principles do not. The series was launched when the study of economic history was burgeoning and new findings and fresh interpretations were threatening to overwhelm students – and sometimes their teachers. The series has expanded its scope, particularly in the area of social history – although the distinction between 'economic' and 'social' is sometimes hard to recognise and even more difficult to sustain. It has also extended geographically; its roots remain firmly British, but an increasing number of titles is concerned with the economic and social history of the wider world. However, some of the early titles can no longer claim to be introductions to the current state of scholarship; and the discipline as a whole lacks the heady growth of the 1960s and early 1970s. To overcome the first problem a number of new editions, or entirely new works, have been commissioned – some have already appeared. To deal with the second, the aim remains to publish up-to-date introductions to important areas of debate. If the series can demonstrate to students and their teachers the importance of the discipline of economic and social history and excite its further study, it will continue the task so ably begun by its first two editors.

The Queen's University of Belfast   L. A. CLARKSON
                                                       General Editor

Acknowledgements

I am very grateful to the following colleagues for reading an earlier draft and being so generous with their advice and support: Dr Eugenio Biagini, Professor Kenneth Brown, Dr Andrew Davies, Dr Jon Lawrence, Dr J. P. Parry, W. G. Runciman, Dr S. R. S. Szreter, Dr Miles Taylor, Dr Pat Thane, Professor F. M. L. Thompson, and Dr J. M. Winter. I would also like to thank Professor L. A. Clarkson for his patient and unobtrusive editing.

Note on References

References in the text within square brackets relate to the items listed alphabetically in the Select Bibliography, followed, where necessary, by the page numbers in italics; for example [Rubinstein, 1981a, *68*].

1 Introduction

Despite important differences in their approach, historians would probably agree that many of the central features which still characterize modern British society were crystallized during the nineteenth century. These would normally include a highly productive economy increasingly integrated by rapid transport, an ever-growing population increasingly resident in urban areas, and a system of government which was increasingly professional and responsive to popular pressure. Although these developments may have rested on the achievements of previous generations, they also seemed to pose unprecedented challenges to the existing structures of power by giving rise to new types of wealth, new forms of popular organization, and new problems of social order. Defining the beginning and the end of this process of transformation is an impossible task, but it would probably also be generally agreed that the mid-nineteenth century marked some sort of turning point, as the new society became increasingly integrated into an effectively functioning whole, and many of the conflicts and pressures which might have threatened its stability seemed to have been successfully resolved.

Since this period is comparatively recent and many of its features are still characteristic of modern life, it is perhaps not surprising that its first historians found some difficulty in establishing an appropriate critical distance from which to assess it. Thus, though their work still contains some of the most suggestive insights into the ideas of the ruling classes and the nature of the British state, Elie Halévy, G. M. Young and Kitson Clark were all noticeably more caught up in the conflicting loyalties of nineteenth century party politics, and more involved in establishing an appropriate emotional response to 'Victorianism', than any student of the period would be today. An important step towards a more detached perspective was made in the 1960s, when historians such as Edward Thompson, Eric Hobsbawm and Harold Perkin began to use categories drawn from

various traditions of the social sciences to develop a more sophisticated analysis of the working classes and to ask new questions about
broad processes of social change. However, the degree of this
detachment should not be exaggerated, as the traditions involved
can themselves be traced back to nineteenth century thinkers such
as Marx, Spencer and Bagehot, and in so far as it was successful,
this project usually depended on a rather deterministic elimination
of precisely that intimate acquaintance with the detail of Victorian
life which had characterized the work of the previous generation.

In the last decade, aided by the passing of time, and by the
important contributions of both of these previous groups of historians,
there has been a growing attempt to combine inquiries into the
ruling classes and the working classes, and to integrate the detailed
contributions of political, cultural and economic history with the
critical analysis of social power. This has involved a revival of many
of the insights of the earlier school of nineteenth century historians,
but the powerful new theories of the 1960s have also continued to
play a large part in setting the research agenda, for though their
categories were rather hard-edged and reductionist, they also had
the virtue of focusing attention on a set of clearly defined questions.
Much of the survey which follows will be concerned with revising
these categories, so it will be helpful to lay them out briefly by way of
introduction, in the form of the simplified diagram of Table 1.1.

Table 1.1   1960s Assumptions about Nineteenth Century Society

Old order to 1790	De-stabilization 1790–1850	New order from 1850
Aristocratic landlords		Bourgeois industrialists
	X	
Independent small farmers/artisans		Subordinate factory proletariat

From this it will be seen that the central assumption of the social
science approach of the 1960s was that there had been a complete
break in the nature of the social order in the early nineteenth century
as a result of the 'Industrial Revolution'. Both because of the trauma
involved in such a fundamental transformation, and because of the

10

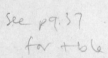

nature of the new social classes which it produced, it was necessary to construct a new set of social relations. For alongside the replacement of independent and dispersed small farmers and artisans by a subordinate and concentrated factory proletariat, there had been a replacement of the traditional landed and paternalistic aristocracy by a more or less ruthless industrial bourgeoisie. Given the inevitable increase in economic class conflict and the recurrent threat of mass popular revolt which resulted, it had therefore been necessary to introduce new methods of social control. As a result, the history of the first half of the nineteenth century was written largely in terms of the threat of dramatic social revolution, while that of the second half was written largely in terms of the success of dull social stabilization.

In the following chapters the major revisions which have been made to all aspects of this approach will be considered in turn, beginning with an assessment of recent research on the nature of the ruling classes, moving on to a similar assessment of recent research on the working classes, and then discussing the increasingly wide range of theories which have been suggested for the analysis of the relations between them.

2   The Ruling Classes

(i) BOURGEOISIE OR ARISTOCRACY?

Given the strength of the assumptions outlined in the Introduction, questioning the idea that Britain was ruled by the industrial bourgeoisie in the second half of the nineteenth century may be surprising to some readers. However, until the early 1960s it was commonly taken for granted that the country had in fact continued to be ruled by the landed aristocracy at least up until the First World War, a view which was especially strong among historians familiar with the substance of national political power [Kitson Clark, 1962; Gash, 1965]. The social science approach which became increasingly influential from the middle of the 1960s argued for the rise of the industrial bourgeoisie, based on their growing economic wealth from the middle of the eighteenth century, their tightening grip on political power in the early nineteenth century, and their successful domination of social values by the middle of the nineteenth century [E. P. Thompson, 1963; Perkin, 1969]. However, as further research has been done in each of these areas it has led to a revival of the previous emphasis on the persistence of the aristocracy. Indeed it is interesting to note the consistent reference, both by historians and by contemporaries, to non-landed property owners as the '*middle* classes' implying that, however wealthy and influential they were becoming in the nineteenth century, there still remained more powerful groups above them in the national hierarchy. Perhaps equally significantly, the standing of the highest income groups within the working classes has often been indicated by referring to them as 'labour *aristocrats*'.

As in any other area of inquiry it is necessary to establish a clear and consistent terminology if progress is to be made, and it has to be said that recent debates on the ruling classes in late nineteenth century Britain have at times become rather bogged down in a

12

shifting use of important labels. For example, despite the obvious implication of the phrase 'middle classes' just referred to, historians who argue for the rise of the bourgeoisie have often used it in ways which imply a reference to the country's dominant social group. Similarly, in assessing the relative weight to be given to landowners and industrialists, these historians have sometimes blurred important lines of distinction by including on the industrial side of the scale, not only the activities of bankers and merchants, but even those of the professions. On the other hand, historians who argue for the persistence of the old elite have sometimes forgotten that, despite the large area of overlap between them, there is a distinction between the economic category of large landowners, and the social and political category of the aristocracy. This sort of confusion has been minimized in the survey which follows, but no doubt there remain issues which require further serious thought and a concerted effort to use important labels more carefully in future discussions.

The enthusiasm generated by the process of rediscovery of the nature of the ruling classes has also often resulted in the new evidence becoming associated with excessive claims followed inevitably by objections, and these controversies have sometimes threatened to confuse the central issues of social analysis. It is therefore important not to assume that the persistence of the aristocracy is the explanation for everything in modern Britain or, on the contrary, that if it can be shown to be an inadequate explanation for some important developments it did not exist. This confusion has arisen particularly in the case of its association with the decline of the British economy, which may indeed have had other and more important causes without undermining the case for the persistence of the aristocracy [Wiener, 1981; Gunn, 1988]. Similarly, although some recent studies have emphasized the small numbers of businessmen who bought large landed estates and have seen the aristocracy as a relatively closed social group, this is not a necessary part of the case for aristocratic power [Rubinstein, 1981b; Stone and Stone, 1984]. Indeed, if it should turn out that the more traditional view of landed classes open to new wealth at their lower levels is still more accurate, this would provide a more plausible background to the continued political predominance of the aristocracy in the second half of the nineteenth century [Kitson Clark, 1962; F. M. L. Thompson, 1963, 1977]. Finally, it should be noted that the case for the persistence of

13

the aristocracy is not an argument that the industrial bourgeoisie was totally without power in nineteenth century Britain, or that it was ineffective in achieving its major goals. Rather it is an argument that it did not become the predominant group within the ruling classes, perhaps indeed because of the relatively limited nature of its ambitions.

(ii) WEALTH-HOLDING

One important advance which has recently been made is the analysis of the relative wealth of different groups of property owners by W. D. Rubinstein, using an extensive collection of quantitative data on two major indicators of wealth-holding: the value of individual property at death as recorded in probate calendars, and the assessments of incomes in different districts made by the Inland Revenue for the purposes of taxation [Rubinstein, 1981a]. Each of these measures is subject to some technical qualification for, even before the imposition of heavy taxes on inherited wealth in the twentieth century, the rich may still have had other reasons to dispose of some of their property before death; and, although tax assessments of the living promise a solution to this problem, the measurement of income by area of residence is likely to undervalue the importance of capital holdings in other districts [Gunn, 1988]. However, these shortcomings in the data would both tend to underestimate levels of wealth; there is no good reason to suppose that they would apply systematically to one type of property owner more than to another; and the gaps between the different types are in any case so wide that the inaccuracies in the data would have to be very serious indeed to change the overall picture. Moreover, since most of the objections to Rubinstein's findings have so far been based on individual cases of large industrial fortunes without any attempt at a recalculation of the distribution of wealth in the country as a whole, his overall conclusions have yet to be challenged effectively. From his data a clear picture emerges in which the wealth of landowners was predominant for longer than many historians have tended to assume while, among the increasingly important non-landed wealth-holders, industrial employers came third behind bankers and merchants, with only 30–40 per cent of

14

non-landed fortunes at their mid-nineteenth century peak [Rubin-stein, 1981a, *68*].

As far as landed wealth is concerned, Rubinstein's figures indicate that until the 1880s over half of the very wealthiest still had the bulk of their property in land. Even as income from agricultural rents began to fall from the 1870s, large landowners were able to increase their incomes from coal and mineral royalties and from urban rents, while landowners of all sizes were able to supplement their incomes by diversifying into commercial and financial activities in the City of London, then experiencing rapid growth due to its emergence as the major service centre for the world economy [F. M. L. Thompson, 1963; Cannadine, 1980; Rubinstein, 1981a].

As a result of this latter development there was also a marked concentration of non-landed wealth in London, particularly the City of London, and this was to be found at the level of the middle classes as well as of the very rich. For example, in terms of the total assessments under Schedule D of the income tax in 1880, London still outweighed the other 28 major urban centres in spite of its smaller overall population [Rubinstein, 1981a, *109*]. Within the industrial regions themselves much the same pattern was repeated: centres of commerce like Liverpool contained the highest general levels of wealth, and even in a city like Manchester only one out of the six recorded millionaires was a cotton manufacturer, the others being bankers and merchants. Even when industrial millionaires began to appear more often at the national level after 1890, they were to be found as frequently in consumer processing such as brewing and cigarette-making as in the major manufacturing sectors [Rubinstein, 1981a, *69, 107, 109*].

Thus despite the undoubted growth of manufacturing employ-ment and of the wealth of employers in the northern industries, their fortunes were only impressive at a small town level. This seems to have been largely the result of the limited nature of their ambitions for prosperous family-based firms, as well as of the greater un-certainty and lower rates of return from productive activity in comparison with landownership and finance, and it was closely connected with manufacturers' general avoidance of heavy fixed investment in plant and equipment. As a result, within the country as a whole the manufacturers were still overshadowed by the land-owning classes, and even within their own regions they generally appeared as junior partners to financial and commercial elites. It is interesting to note how well this fits in with recent trends in economic history, which now tends to emphasize a pattern of long, slow growth of British manufacturing, generally small in scale, labour rather than capital intensive, and emerging within the context of an already expanding commercial economy [Crafts, 1985]. This would tend to imply a greater degree of general social continuity than that normally associated with the idea of a dramatic 'Industrial Revolution', and interestingly enough is itself once again a restatement of themes which were more widely recognized in economic history up until the early 1960s [Cole, 1952; Cannadine 1984].

(iii) POLITICAL POWER

In some contrast to this new interest in patterns of wealth-holding, there has been less research recently on issues of political power, such as who held important positions, and in whose interests public policy was formulated. Here the central studies are still F. M. L. Thompson's comprehensive account of landed society and W. G. Guttsman's analysis of the national political elite [F. M. L. Thompson, 1963; Guttsman, 1963]. These studies show that it is important not to take the 1832 Reform Act as an index of the rise to power of the industrial bourgeoisie for, although the new franchise did increase the representation of the urban middle classes, it was also designed to reduce the power of newly wealthy owners of corrupt boroughs and to restore the traditional influence of the landed elite: as late as the 1860s almost two-thirds of the country's MPs came from landed backgrounds, over one-third of them were hereditary aristocrats, and around half of the cabinets of both parties were still aristocratic [F. M. L. Thompson, 1963; Guttsman, 1963, *40–1, 78, 82*]. The first major changes in the nature of the political elite only began after the second Reform Act of 1867 which, by extending the franchise to certain layers of the urban working classes, began to replace local patterns of influence with professionally organized political machines. This was a slow process but it had a significant effect on the role of landowners and aristocrats in politics, and it was accelerated not only by further extensions of the franchise but also by such reforms as the Secret Ballot Act of 1872, the restriction of candidates' spending on elections by the 1883 Corrupt Practices Act, the dilution of the aristocracy through awards of peerages in recognition of wealth and political service which began in 1885, and the establishment of elections for local government in the counties in 1888.

Given the parallel decline in revenues from agriculture and the increasing importance of urban landholdings and financial activities for the wealth of the upper classes, it is probably fair to talk of a major restructuring of the British Establishment from the 1870s. This was the period of fruition of the reform of the public schools and Oxbridge; of the integration of the higher professions into the gentlemanly elite and the professionalization of the civil service and the armed forces; and of the creation of the modern constitutional monarchy and the formal British Empire [Young, 1936; Kitson Clark, 1962]. However, it is important to note that this was also the time at which provincial manufacturers' share of the national wealth began to decline from its mid-century peak, and that the restructuring of the Establishment did not give them a greatly enhanced position of power at the national level [Rubinstein, 1981a]. Membership of the ruling circles was being extended to include larger numbers of bankers and merchants but only a few manufacturers, and the great country houses were beginning to be displaced from the centre of political power by more formal institutions of socialization and social contact, if anything based even more firmly in the south of the country. This new network of power and influence thus continued to be based for at least another generation on the aristocracy, as a result of its enormous inherited wealth and its entrenched social and political prestige. Though it no longer dominated British society as a whole to anything like the extent it had done in the early nineteenth century, the aristocracy still remained the leading group within the ruling classes, and it continued to fill half the places and all the top positions in the cabinets of both political parties [F. M. L. Thompson, 1963; Guttsman, 1963; F. M. L. Thompson, 1977].

Of course, analysing political power simply in terms of who filled the main positions is open to the objection that it tells us nothing of how and in whose interests they acted, and it could be argued that the industrial bourgeoisie was able to exert enough pressure on the nation's political elite to get the kind of government it wanted

17

[Perkin, 1969]. However, the challenge to which the restructuring of the Establishment had been a response seems to have come less from industrial employers than from the growth of occupationally-based pressure groups among both the professional middle classes and the working classes, which had been able to win major reforms in the 1860s and 1870s and were to make further important advances in the 1890s and 1900s [Perkin, 1989]. It is true that after the 1832 Reform Act the Lancashire factory owners became a substantial group in the House of Commons, but their effectiveness was limited by internal political divisions and by their inability to create external alliances with other parliamentary groupings. Over the long term the factory owners tended to become less active in politics, more conservative in their social behaviour, and more strongly attached to the Tory party, the traditional political organization of the Lancashire aristocracy [Joyce, 1980; Howe, 1984].

The one apparent assertion of industrial against landed interests was the Repeal of the Corn Laws in 1846 which, by allowing the free importation of foreign corn, eventually led to a long-term fall in the price of domestic corn and thus threatened the profits of British farmers. Here, however, is the crux of the matter, for it was the tenant farmers who stood to suffer most, while landowners were under no obligation to reduce their rent demands in anticipation of a fall in their tenants' incomes. While Repeal was advantageous to the manufacturers, who had a direct interest in cheaper food to keep wage costs down, it is therefore not so clear that it was immediately disadvantageous to the landowners, much of whose land was devoted to pastoral farming, and whose rents from arable land were in any case largely maintained for the duration of the long mid-century boom [F. M. L. Thompson, 1963]. Moreover the Anti-Corn Law League itself should be seen as a popular radical campaign which secured an unusual amount of financial backing from manufacturers because of the economic benefits they expected [Grampp, 1960; Howe, 1984]; and the repeal of the Corn Laws should be seen as a result of aristocratic concession to popular opinion during a short-term crisis, rather than of the long-term growth of bourgeois political power [Kitson Clark, 1962; Gash, 1965]. Otherwise it would be hard to explain why it should have been followed the very next year by a significant limitation of the hours of work in factories, in the face of strong opposition from most of the Lancashire manufacturers [Howe, 1984]; and why it should have been another twenty years before the next instalment of parliamentary reform, despite its energetic promotion by such a prominent Anti-Corn Law leader as John Bright [Kitson Clark, 1962].

A similar pattern can be seen, not only in the widespread aristocratic support for the agricultural labourers' demands in the 1870s, but also in government attitudes towards labour policy in general throughout the period. While trade unions had been illegal under emergency wartime legislation from 1799 to 1824, and were still subject to major penalties under both civil and criminal law thereafter, as they were able to mount increasingly effective pressure in the mid-nineteenth century their demands were met with major concessions from above. Thus in 1871 and 1875 parliamentary legislation gave the unions a series of immunities from the common law over matters such as liability for damages actions, the right to picket, and the status of collective funds, and in 1875 the inequitable provisions of the Master and Servant Act were repealed [Brown, 1982]. Thereafter the main line of government policy on industrial relations was the broadly liberal one of not only recognizing but even strengthening the rights of employees to bargain collectively over wages and working conditions: for example, by pressing railway and shipping employers to accept trade unions in the 1900s, and by restating and extending union immunities under the 1906 Trade Disputes Act [Davidson, 1978]. Once again, then, it had been possible for Britain's ruling elite, based as it was on landownership, commerce and increasingly on overseas finance, to maintain social stability through liberal concessions to pressure from below without having to sacrifice its own immediate political and economic interests [Fox, 1985; Mandler, 1990].

There has, however, been a reaction against this renewed emphasis on the marginal position of manufacturers within the British ruling classes by emphasizing instead their power within local communities in the industrial regions [Howe, 1984; Trainor, 1985; and for earlier examples, see Foster, 1974 and Joyce, 1980]. Given their wealth and their influence as employers it would indeed be surprising if they had not exercised considerable local power, but what is striking about most of the recent research is rather its emphasis on the limits to that power, at least within the political arena. In the first place, there was a clear counterweight to the provision of employment in the development of towns and that was the ownership of land: aristocratic influence persisted in many industrial towns until at least the 1870s [Cannadine, 1980]. In the second place there were other competing non-landed groups, above all the mercantile, retailing and professional middle classes, who were in general more active in local government than manufacturers [Hennock, 1973]. Even the unusually high level of involvement of factory owners in politics in Lancashire went into decline after 1850, partly because of the satisfaction of their ambitions for status, and partly because of the growth in the size of the towns and in th importance of other groups among the local middle classes. Thus whereas in the 1840s over 50 per cent of the town councillors in Bolton and Salford had been manufacturers, this had already fallen to under 40 per cent by the 1870s, and it continued to decline thereafter [Garrard, 1983, *13–23*]. In Manchester itself the liberal manufacturers had been dependent even in their heyday on the electoral support of artisans and retailers, and from the 1860s it was this 'shopocracy' which began to dominate in local office holding [Gatrell, 1982].

It seems likely, then, that the political predominance of the manufacturers would have been confined to the smaller industrial towns and that even there it would not have been unlimited. After all, the powers of local government were acquired either by special private bills which had to be approved by parliament, or by national permissive acts which generally required the establishment of more democratic local procedures [Prest, 1990]. Moreover, local execution came to depend increasingly on professional council officers, and the manufacturers themselves remained internally divided over politics and subject to increasingly effective pressure from the working classes [Garrard, 1983].

(iv) CULTURAL INFLUENCE

Despite its relatively lowly status in terms of wealth-holding and political power, it might still be argued that, as a dynamic, rising class, the industrial bourgeoisie had a cultural influence disproportionate to its economic and political base. In this way it could still be seen as a leading or 'hegemonic' class, not in need of direct rule or

20

influence because it was able to shape policy through its impact on the attitudes and values of the country as a whole, moulding society in its own image and indirectly influencing the behaviour of the more prominent actors, who were after all themselves major property owners [Perkin, 1969; Gray, 1977]. Much of the discussion of these issues has run into serious difficulties in defining what is to be understood by 'bourgeois' as opposed to 'aristocratic' values, for it clearly makes little sense to regard the bourgeoisie as a group with an exclusively economic set of attitudes, or to regard the aristocracy as uninterested in the accumulation of wealth. It is also unclear how exactly the effectiveness of cultural influence on society at large is to be measured, and some of the best known studies are still rather impressionistic in their approach [Coleman, 1973; Wiener, 1981]. To make the problem more manageable it is probably better to avoid such currently intractable general problems and to focus on the simpler question of whether the specific interests of manufacturers were represented in the attitudes and values of the ruling elite.

If a country's literary culture can be taken as an index of the concerns of its rulers it is clear that in Britain manufacturers, far from reshaping dominant attitudes, were consistently rejected unless they conformed to existing social values. In a recent survey Neil McKendrick has suggested that literary attitudes towards business-men were directly related to their perceived economic success and consequent fears of the disruption of the social order. Up until the 1760s attitudes were ambiguous, but thereafter the trend was distinctly towards literary condemnation of new wealth, reaching a peak in the rejection of provincial manufacturers between the 1840s and the 1930s. Within literary treatments of these issues the only route to acceptance was to adopt the values of civilized culture and public service associated with the gentleman, and later the pro-fessional man, and to abandon the values of mere money-making and sectional interest associated with new wealth [McKendrick, 1986; see also Williams, 1958]. This picture is confirmed by studies of the country's elite educational institutions, the public schools and Oxbridge: in so far as they shifted from a predominantly classical literary education towards an increasing acceptance of the natural sciences and a direct interest in public policy in the late nineteenth century, this took place under the influence of professional values and they continued to produce graduates with a strong preference for careers in government, the higher professions, and the financial sector [Kitson Clarke, 1962; Coleman, 1973; Wiener, 1981; Perkin, 1989].

These elite values undoubtedly had an effect on the industrial bourgeoisie itself: many of its members lived in town houses or holidayed at coastal resorts located on large landed estates; most of them aspired to acceptance by the Establishment, and the wealthier among them sent their sons to public schools and bought their own landed estates; those of them who became active in political life did so in parties led by the aristocracy [F. M. L. Thompson, 1963; Coleman, 1973; Cannadine, 1980; Morris, 1990]. There is, however, still room for disagreement on the relevance for subjective attitudes of such outward behaviour, and it is also clear that there was a significant space for the cultural influence of non-landed groups within the industrial regions. What is not so clear is that this space was filled by a culture directly reflecting the interests of the industrial bourgeoisie, for recent studies have begun to uncover a picture similar to that already indicated for local government: merchants, retailers, and professionals were just as active, if not more so, than manufacturers, and there were important political and religious divisions within local middle classes [D. Smith, 1982; Wolff and Seed, 1988; Morris, 1990].

The most plausible counter-argument for the influence of the industrial bourgeoisie on national values emphasizes the increasing centrality of the market and the language of economics, or 'political economy' as it was often called in the nineteenth century [Gunn, 1988]. It is, however, ultimately unconvincing to link this set of ideas to the specific interests of manufacturers since it was first systematically developed by David Hume and Adam Smith in the milieu of the Scottish country gentry, and it was derived more from liberal philosophical and political concerns than as a projection of sectional interests [Grampp, 1960; Fox, 1985]. Indeed, over the long run, the commitment to free trade and open competition seems to have been stronger among domestic consumers and overseas financiers than among British manufacturers who, like most of their foreign counterparts, generally preferred to sell where they had a built-in advantage [Green, 1988]. It is also difficult to see political economy as representing in some looser way the interests of the propertied classes as a whole: it encountered strong opposition from other values, above all Evangelical Christianity with its stress on the need for moral behaviour and social justice on the part of the rulers; it was abandoned in practice when middle-class voluntary associations gave financial subsidies to those local cultural activities they wished to promote; and indeed it was itself successfully adapted by the working classes in their pursuit of more effective collective bargaining arrangements [Halévy, 1924; Young, 1936; Biagini, 1987; Morris, 1990].

These points underline the enormous difficulties involved in attaching ideas and values exclusively to particular social groups and suggest that it is better to see them as the result of long historical developments, affected by specific events and by the competing political and religious affiliations which emerged from them, rather than directly reflecting the material interests of social classes. The importance of conservatism and the emphasis on continuity will already be obvious; it had deep roots in the reaction to the domestic disaster of the Civil War in the seventeenth century, and it was reinforced by the foreign threat of the French Revolution after 1789. Indeed, it is probably more accurate to see the strong sense of unease about social stability in the first half of the nineteenth century as a product of the observation of European political events more than of social restructuring and the threat of social revolution within Britain itself. This provoked a strongly anti-democratic reaction and a range of schemes for the promotion of cultural elites which can be found in all parts of the political spectrum and which deeply influenced the outlook of the later Victorian generations [Williams, 1958]. Yet at the same time, conservative values faced strong competition from liberal ones, which also had deep roots in the seventeenth century, this time in the struggles for religious freedom, the advances in scientific thinking, and the beginnings of the secular Enlightenment. If anything, the roots of liberal values were deeper and stronger in Britain: to be found in the long tradition of the English common law, formulated by local social interaction rather than by central state intervention; and in the long struggle of parliament and the aristocracy against the power of the monarchy, which was finally settled by the 'Glorious Revolution' of 1689 [Halévy, 1924; Fox, 1985]. Thus, in so far as there were values after 1850 which corresponded to the interests of the industrial bourgeoisie, they pre-dated and facilitated its emergence rather than being created by, and belonging exclusively to, that one social group. Moreover, while those values supported individual economic enterprise they also set limits to it: conservatism insisted that change be gradual, and liberalism insisted that the rights of all citizens be respected [Young, 1936].

Some historians have attempted to restore the picture of a neatly divided two-class society by suggesting that all groups of property owners were increasingly integrated into a new ruling class after 1850 [Trainor, 1985; Gunn, 1988]. However, given the weight of evidence on the different economic functions, different geographical locations, and different access to wealth and power of the groups involved, as well as the absence of a unifying world-view, this will need more precision and more empirical support before it can be established as a viable case. In the meantime the above discussion of the ruling classes indicates that it makes little sense to see British society in this period as polarized between an industrial bourgeoisie and an industrial proletariat. For the existence of a national political elite based on the landowning, financial, and commercial classes meant that economic conflicts between capital and labour could be mediated by concessions which often encroached on the interests of employers in both industry and agriculture. Paradoxically, there was at the same time considerable room for agreement between capital and labour in attacking the political monopoly of the aristocracy, an agreement which was frequently reinforced by shared local, political, and religious loyalties. These shifting alliances within a three-cornered relationship should already begin to make more sense of the history of the period, but the way they have so far been presented has taken the nature of the relationship between capital and labour rather for granted. It is therefore now time to look in more detail at the position of the industrial working classes.

3   The Working Classes

It will probably not be surprising to find that in looking at the working classes in Britain after 1850 the central issues to be dealt with are still those which were pursued by Karl Marx. For while Marx's views on the development of modern society have had a significant impact on social history in general, most historians in the Marxist tradition have concentrated on the working classes, and between them they produced some of the most influential research in this field in the 1960s and 1970s. In Marx's analysis the factory proletariat being formed in nineteenth century Britain was a fundamentally new phenomenon: for the first time in history working people were becoming a homogeneous mass of propertyless labourers, brought together in ever larger concentrations, and increasingly sharing a common position at the lowest levels of skill and income:

> with the development of industry the proletariat not only increases in number; it becomes concentrated in greater masses, its strength grows, and it feels that strength more. The various interests and conditions of life within the ranks of the proletariat are more and more equalized, in proportion as machinery obliterates all distinctions of labour, and nearly everywhere reduces wages to the same low level. [K. Marx and F. Engels, 'Manifesto of the Communist Party' (1848), in *Collected Works. Volume VI* (1976), p. 492]

Thus, for Marx, out of the economic development of capitalism itself a working class was being formed which would necessarily be involved in fierce conflict with its employers, and which would have a direct material interest in creating a new society based on public property and absolute equality.

Marx's views on these questions began with a desire to link his ideal future society to a historical process which he could claim was already under way, rather than with an empirical study of the detailed conditions of life of British workers, and the resulting inheritance for his followers has been a problematic one. The orthodox position is that the formation of the industrial proletariat leads to the emergence of revolutionary class consciousness, which then has to be contained by an effective ruling class response if the social order is not to be overturned [Hobsbawm, 1949; Foster, 1974]. However, the general absence of revolutionary socialism among modern British workers has led to the development of a less orthodox, but more widespread, position that it is the trauma of being turned into a proletariat which creates revolutionary possibilities, and that it is therefore rebellious skilled workers who have to be contained by an effective ruling class response [E. P. Thompson, 1963; R. Price, 1980]. This in turn can then be developed logically to the most unorthodox position that, once the resistance of skilled workers has been overcome, the proletariat proper becomes an acquiescent and resigned social group, not in need of any special measures of containment [Stedman Jones, 1975; Joyce, 1980]. It is striking that each of these three distinct approaches is based on the same central assumption of a process of de-skilling within modern industry, whether seen as leading to proletarian class consciousness, to revolutionary resistance among skilled workers, or to a de-politicized working class. It is also striking that all three approaches have involved the development of explanations of the effective subordination of the working classes, however they have assessed the nature of the political threat to the social order. As a result, the assumption that modern industry leads to a loss of skill and an increasingly homogeneous working class, which is potentially revolutionary but in practice politically subordinate, has been very widespread in the social history of the period, whether explicitly Marxist or not [Perkin, 1969].

More recently, however, historians initially stimulated by the central role in the development of modern society given by Marx to de-skilling, have begun to look in more detail at the organization and conditions of work in British industry, with the result that a revised view is beginning to emerge. By examining more closely the role of trade unions, the nature of technical innovation, and the

26

substance of employers' approaches to labour management, this view suggests that the extent of de-skilling has at least been exaggerated, and may indeed have been the opposite of what was happening. As a result, industrial workers are now generally seen as having been less effectively subordinated to the domination of their employers and as having retained a wider variety of experiences and attitudes. And it is interesting to note that, as in the case of the ruling classes discussed in the previous chapter, this both fits in well with the recent re-emphasis by economic historians on the gradual nature of industrial change, and also amounts to the revival of a view of the working classes themselves which was more widely held before the 1960s [Cole, 1952, 1955; Crafts, 1985].

(ii) SKILLS

The first problem with the assumption of an inevitable tendency towards de-skilling is that it does not leave any space for the possibility of effective resistance by skilled workers. This was a widespread objection among Marxists themselves to the restatement of Marx's theory in an unrevised version in the 1970s, and as a result there is now a broad consensus, even among those who still see a long-run tendency towards de-skilling and subordination, that well-organized groups of workers can not only rebel but can also delay and modify these pressures [Samuel, 1977; Gray, 1981; Wood, 1982].

This has been demonstrated very pertinently for Britain in the second half of the nineteenth century by William Lazonick's study of changes in technology and the work process among Lancashire cotton spinners [Lazonick, 1979]. This, of course, is a key case because, even when it is conceded that conditions in more traditional sectors may have been different, it is usually assumed that the long-run tendencies of industrial economies will be seen most clearly in their most highly mechanized sectors. However, it appears that, even after the introduction of the 'automatic' or 'self-acting' mule in the early nineteenth century, which largely displaced the skilled physical effort that had previously been required, the adult spinners within the work groups retained real autonomy because they still had to use some physical aptitude in overseeing the routine opera-

27

tion of the equipment and they still had to supervise the labour of their assistants, or 'piecers', who were responsible for tying up the broken threads. Some Marxist historians have argued that this outcome was deceptive: the result either of employers' imposition of a new elite of supervisors on a totally de-skilled workforce, or of their toleration of now out-dated status distinctions within a workforce in reality uniformly subordinated by the new technology [Foster, 1974; Stedman Jones, 1975]. However, Lazonick's more detailed account suggests that the outcome was in fact based firstly on employers' preference for continuing to rely on already established spinner-piecer relationships as their method of supervision for the new equipment, and secondly on the effectiveness of the Lancashire spinners' resistance to employers' later pressure for other forms of work organization, such as those involving larger work groups and female labour which were adopted in Scotland. Thus the spinners' union continued to be able to make significant gains for its members throughout the second half of the nineteenth century, especially over wages and work-speeds, and its control over the division of labour was one of the factors which discouraged employers from a more widespread adoption of the new ring spinning machinery towards the end of the period [Lazonick, 1979].

This case would suggest then, that far from shaping their work-forces entirely at their own discretion, British employers tended to adapt their management methods to existing work practices and to the preferences of their workers' organizations. If this was the case even in a highly mechanized sector, engaged in the indoor process-ing of a simple and fairly uniform product, the difficulties which em-ployers had in less mechanized, less easily supervised, and more complex production situations can easily be imagined. Thus recent work on coal mining, the traditional crafts in housebuilding, and the new crafts in metal working has all tended to stress the contribution of trade unionism to the protection of high levels of skill and auton-omy on the job, and it should, of course, be remembered that less mechanized sectors like these still provided the vast bulk of employ-ment in the period [Harrison, 1978; Harrison and Zeitlin, 1985; McClelland and Reid, 1985; Zeitlin, 1985].

If part of British workers' ability to retain a position of skill and independence was due to the effective resistance of their trade unions, another part of the explanation is to be found in the inherent

28

limits of technology itself. Academics often write as if new technology were all-powerful in its ability to displace the human input to production, for this is a widespread cultural assumption in industrial societies and it is rare for scholars to have had direct experience of the complexities of industrial labour. Moreover, the original promoters of new machinery always have a vested interest in exaggerating its capacities, and the trade unions confronted by it are always concerned about its implications, so there is usually plenty of evidence that can be used to suggest that mechanization was accompanied by traumatic de-skilling. However, as surveys of work processes and skill levels in late nineteenth century British industry have increasingly shown, closer analysis of the actual tasks involved rarely confirms such general assumptions [Samuel, 1977; More, 1980].

In the first place machinery was rarely fully automatic: even in the case of the so-called 'self-acting' mule it has already been seen that the spinners still had to put in their own physical effort and supervisory experience if the machinery and the work groups were to operate effectively. Most other cases of apparently automatic equipment required even more skill than this, involving a knowledge of the different capacities of machines, and of the appropriate machines and running speeds for different raw materials. In general the human input displaced by machinery was usually the physical effort involved in strenuous or repetitive tasks, which could be done more quickly and more efficiently by the mechanical application of natural energy resources, while human mental effort was still required for the more skilled parts of the job [Samuel, 1977]. As a result it was common practice to move operators between machines in order to increase their experience and range of knowledge: printing presses and sawing machines provide good examples of this in the case of previously skilled work, while the introduction of powerful haulage equipment provides an interesting example in the case of previously unskilled work. The latter was indeed to become one of the most significant forms of labour-saving in British industry in the early twentieth century, replacing brute physical effort with a demand for semi-skilled work on the part of the crane drivers and other mechanical operators. Moreover, even in cases where machinery resulted in the displacement of skilled workers by new grades of semi-skilled labour, it was always accompanied by parallel increases

29

in the need for other highly skilled workers to build, repair, set up, and supervise the new equipment. Thus the almost universal expression of communal pride in occupational abilities which is to be found in this period stemmed not from old habits or new delusions, but rather from the reality of acquired skill which was still to be found at all levels of the manual workforce [More, 1980].

While the resistance of trade unions and the inherent limits of technology provided two significant barriers to any tendency towards de-skilling, the most important explanation for the high levels of skill and independence among the British working classes probably lies in the attitudes of their employers. Marxists have generally argued not only that capital was inevitably committed to de-skilling, but that its main motivation was less a straightforwardly economic one than a desire to establish effective political and social control over labour [Foster, 1974; Stedman Jones, 1975]. Recent research, however, has shown that the opposite was generally the case: employers were primarily committed to economic profitability, and in Britain their routes to this goal rarely resulted in de-skilling.

This was partly a result of their own organizational weakness, for specialization in different products and divergent attitudes towards labour management could greatly obstruct the internal unity of apparently powerful employers' organizations [Zeitlin, 1985]. However, behind this lay a general lack of interest among British employers in either intensive mechanization or fundamental reorganization of the division of labour: instead there was a marked preference for labour intensive methods and a heavy reliance on largely independent groups of highly skilled workers. By minimizing their investment in plant and machinery employers were able to keep their capital overheads low in an economy notoriously open to the pressures of the world market and subject to sharp seasonal and cyclical fluctuations [Samuel, 1977; McClelland and Reid, 1985]. By contracting-out the training, supervision, quality control, and provision of welfare benefits to the largely self-regulating groups of skilled workers and their trade unions, they were able to make substantial savings on the administrative overheads of labour management [Lazonick, 1979; Melling, 1980]. Finally, by employing skilled workers on multi-purpose equipment they were able to retain maximum flexibility and to follow their long-standing preferences for high quality specialized products [Samuel, 1977; Zeitlin, 1985].

Thus while even workers employed in highly mechanized sectors like cotton spinning retained some skills and some autonomy on the job, late nineteenth century British industry more typically relied on craftsmen and other highly skilled workers who retained considerable levels of technical knowledge and manual ability and who carried out their tasks with a minimum of managerial interference: whenever competitive pressures required that labour costs be reduced this was generally achieved by cutting their wages.

(iii) INCOMES

The recent focus of research on the work process has led to something of a neglect of the more traditional subjects of wages and incomes, though no doubt this is also due to the absence of serious controversy over standards of living in these years. Most observers at the time and since are agreed that the overall trend from mid-century was upwards, by as much as 90 per cent in real wages between 1850 and 1900, at a time when standard hours of work were being reduced by up to 20 per cent [Benson, 1989; 39–56]. However, a number of qualifications to this picture ought to be noted. In the first place, a large part of the improvement in average wages was due to a shift of the workforce towards the better paid occupations, so that not all workers benefited by the same amount and the substantial numbers remaining outside the more prosperous sectors were still seriously disadvantaged [Hopkins, 1975; Benson, 1989]. In the second place, the estimates of wage increases are based either on standard rates or on employers' returns of average earnings and not on the take-home pay of actual individuals, which could be significantly less in cases of workers rated at lower levels or subject to seasonal and cyclical under-employment: it is important to note that these factors regularly reduced the incomes of even the most skilled groups [Hopkins, 1975; Gray, 1976; S. Price, 1981]. Finally, it has become increasingly clear that there was no direct correlation between money incomes and standards of living, for the latter also depended on individual men's choices about spending, especially on drink, as well as individual women's abilities as household managers [Reid, 1983; Roberts, 1984; Davies, 1991].

It is therefore important not to exaggerate the improvements in living standards over this period: as Henry Pelling has pointed out, even the increasingly 'comfortable' upper half of the working classes still had to cope with large families, poor housing, accidents, illness and periodic unemployment, while among the poorer half many were truly destitute [Pelling, 1968a; see also Benson, 1989]. Indeed, the most interesting recent research in this field has been done by oral historians, who have emphasized the limited nature of improvements in material standards of living before the First World War, and who have highlighted the energy and resourcefulness with which working people coped with their constrained circumstances, whether in the form of housewives 'making ends meet', or of men and women 'passing the time' after work [Tebbutt, 1983; Roberts, 1984; Davies, 1991].

However, even if the individual experience of the quality of life was generally still a grim one, there can be little doubt that the overall trend in incomes was still upwards and that this implies a long-run increase in the economic, social, and political independence of the working classes. Some Marxists, following suggestions made by Frederick Engels, have attempted to maintain their overall emphasis on the formation of a subordinate proletariat by restricting the acknowledgement of this improvement in conditions to a small upper stratum, or 'labour aristocracy', of 10 per cent of the working classes [Hobsbawm, 1954; Gray, 1976]. However, this seems increasingly implausible as more evidence is gathered on the growing ability of all types of worker to pay small sums of money into collective funds of one sort or another after meeting more pressing personal needs [Johnson, 1985]. Indeed, as Henry Pelling has emphasized, friendly societies and co-operative retailing societies spread well beyond the ranks of the most skilled and best paid throughout the period; the less skilled occupations were increasingly able to sustain trade union organization, especially after 1889; and the skilled and unskilled unions collaborated in establishing the Labour party in 1900 [Pelling, 1968a; see also Kirk, 1985, and F. M. L. Thompson, 1988]. Even among rural labourers recent research has highlighted significant improvements in standards of living, as de-casualization and rural depopulation accelerated after 1870, and increasingly effective self-organization, especially following the revival of agricultural trade unionism in the 1900s [Howkins, 1985]. Only if it is argued that these activities and organizations made no difference at all, and that those involved in them had been deluded into wasting their time and money, can it seriously be maintained that there was no significant increase in the independence of the working classes as a whole over the period.

Interestingly enough, recent research on another major group in the population which has been viewed for some time mainly in terms of its increasing subordination is also beginning to re-emphasize important areas of growing independence. For women too this was a period of improved standards of living and health, with particularly direct benefits coming from reductions in family size, as well as a gradually widening range of occupational opportunities. It was also a period of growing legal rights in the areas of marriage, child custody, property ownership and working conditions. And it was a period of increasingly effective women's self-organization in the work place, in trade unions and friendly societies, in educational institutions, and in local and national politics [Roberts, 1988; Thane, 1988].

A further important objection to the notion of a small elite sitting above a homogeneous mass of increasingly impoverished labour arises out of the new approach to the work process described in the previous section. Since there was no clear-cut tendency towards de-skilling and the simplification of industrial tasks, but rather the continued predominance of a wide range of types and levels of skilled labour, it is natural to expect that this would have been accompanied by complex hierarchies of wages corresponding to the supply of, and the demand for, the various types of skill required by employers. This is indeed exactly what emerges from most studies of wages and earnings in particular industries, which highlight the unsatisfactory nature of any simple division within the working classes, whether between 'labour aristocrats' and 'plebeians', between skilled and unskilled labour, or between men and women. Instead it appears that most workers found themselves on complex wage ladders with many steps along which they generally expected to move, in both directions, at different stages in their working lives [Gray, 1981; Roberts, 1988].

Moreover, taken together, a number of recent studies suggest that vertical divisions between industries and occupations may have had more influence on working class attitudes and organizations than horizontal divisions between income strata. One of the most important of these vertical divisions was that between industries in which training was given through the craft apprenticeship of teen-agers, and industries in which training was acquired by a lifetime of experience on the job [More, 1980]. On the one hand, in the craft industries, such as engineering and shipbuilding, there were signific-ant numbers of adult workers who were permanently excluded from the most skilled jobs, who eventually formed their own separate occupationally-based trade unions paralleling those of the crafts-men, and who were able to win wage increases leading to income overlaps with the lower end of the skilled trades [S. Price, 1981; McClelland and Reid, 1985]. On the other hand, in the seniority sectors, such as coal mining, cotton spinning, and glass-making, most adults could aspire to the top jobs, the majority of workers were organized within the same industry-based trade unions, and a strict hierarchy of income grades was maintained through internal union discipline [Matsumura, 1983]. Morever, craft workers, having in principle acquired a full training by the age of twenty-one, could and did move freely between firms and districts in search of better pay, while seniority workers generally had to stay in one particular workplace if they were to move up the job and wage ladders

These differences in the patterns of training, wages, mobility and trade union structure had important wider consequences for working-class organization and attitudes [Cole, 1937; Pelling, 1967, 1968a; Tanner, 1990]. The craft unions, with their effective control of highly skilled and highly mobile occupations, conducted their industrial actions in the form of small-scale strikes in particular workplaces, which generally both brought them better results in terms of wages and conditions, and left them with large financial balances to support their members in periods of unemployment, sickness and retirement. When they took an interest in parliamen-tary politics it was usually with the aim of minimizing government interference in industrial affairs: it was they who led the successful pressure on the Liberal party for the reform of the labour laws in the 1870s, and it was largely the same motivation which lay behind their affiliation to the Labour party in the 1900s. This long tradition of libertarianism could also sometimes provide a fertile environment for pockets of more revolutionary anti-state attitudes, most notably in the Glasgow metal working industries in the early twentieth century [McLean, 1983; J. Smith, 1984; Reid, 1985]. The seniority

34

unions, with their wider bases in regionally concentrated industries, were more inclined to conduct their industrial actions in the form of district-wide or industry-wide mass strikes, which did not always bring success and considerably weakened their ability to provide continuous welfare benefits. As a result they generally had a stronger interest in securing government support in industrial and welfare matters, especially as their regional concentration and residential stability gave them a good deal of political influence within particular constituencies. The best known examples of this were the cotton workers' successful pressure on the Conservative party for factory legislation in the 1840s, and the building up from the 1880s of a large and effective group of Liberal miners' MPs: when these groups eventually joined the Labour party they were therefore generally more active in pushing for state intervention [Tanner, 1990].

Thus, just as in the case of the ruling classes, there were important vertical divisions within the working classes, arising from the nature of their economic activity. However, it should no more be assumed in the case of the latter than in the case of the former that their attitudes were shaped solely by economic influences: it has just been noted for example, that seniority workers' pursuit of government support could be compatible with either Liberalism or Conservatism. Once again then, a complete historical analysis would need to include the independent influence of ideas and values, shaped as they were by historical events and by local political and religious loyalties which frequently cut across the categories of economic analysis [Halévy, 1924; Reid, 1983; Howkins, 1985; Biagini and Reid, 1991]. Thus part of the explanation for the miners' attachment to Liberalism in contrast to the cotton workers' strong Conservatism is to be found in the strength of Methodism in the coal fields in contrast to that of Anglicanism in Lancashire [Harrison, 1978; Joyce, 1980].

Despite a variety of attempts to update the Marxist approach to the analysis of the British working classes, it seems increasingly inappropriate to see their history as one of the long-term reduction of their skills and incomes to the lowest common denominator, with each stage of increasing homogeneity being accompanied by a new form of effective subordination to their employers [Foster, 1974;

35

Stedman Jones, 1975; Joyce, 1980; R. Price, 1980]. Rather, most working men and women throughout the period 1850 to 1914 retained real skills and real autonomy at work, experienced a rising trend of real incomes, and were increasingly able to sustain their own independent economic, social and political organizations. As a result, the inevitability of fierce conflict between capital and labour was considerably reduced and there were many areas where agreement was possible, even over the organization of work itself. Morever, the diversity of skills and incomes reduces the plausibility of explanations of popular attitudes based on horizontal strata and indicates that the exploration of vertical divisions may be more productive. This would open up the question of differences within the Liberal and Labour parties, provide a basis for the understanding of the strength of working-class Conservatism in particular occupations and regions, and act as a continual reminder that wider popular movements always involve the construction of alliances between sections of the working classes with distinct experiences, ambitions and values.

4 Social Relations

(i) DOMINATION OR AGREEMENT?

The discussion of the nature of the ruling classes and the working classes in the last two chapters implies that some revisions ought to be made to Table 1.1 in the Introduction, which laid out the assumptions established in the field in the 1960s. It now seems that it would be more accurate to summarize the picture of British society after 1850 as in Table 4.1.

Table 4.1   Revised Assumptions about Nineteenth Century Society

'Old order' to 1790	Continuity 1790–1850	'New order' from 1850
Aristocratic landlords		Aristocratic landlords/financiers
Independent small farmers/artisans	⟶	Independent skilled workers

Clearly this suggests a greater degree of continuity in the nature of the major social classes throughout the nineteenth century than has often been assumed. Moreover, the questioning of the existence of a major social crisis in the early nineteenth century which is also suggested, parallels the recent revision of the notion of a dramatic 'Industrial Revolution' among economic historians. A good deal of thought, however, still needs to be paid to how to characterize the undoubted processes of change which were taking place in the course of the nineteenth century. It would be misleading to point only to continuity: over these years Britain was transformed from a largely rural to a largely urban society, within which levels both of population and of material consumption reached unprecedented heights. It would be equally misleading to ignore the serious stresses and strains which accompanied this transformation: above all as a result of the combined pressure of all groups within the urban population for new forms of freedom and self-government. However, while the results were unprecedented, the means by which they had been achieved were not: much of the new wealth and power had accumulated in the same old hands, above all those of landlords and financiers, and much of the new productivity had been achieved less by heavy investment in science-based technology, and more by piecemeal innovation and the reorganization of a largely skilled labour force. Thus while there had been 'revolutionary' changes in British society, the fact that these had not been accompanied by a violent political revolution probably had less to do with their containment by the construction of a new set of social relations, and more to do with their containment by a significant degree of continuity in the established set of social relations [Halévy, 1924; Young, 1936; Kitson Clark, 1962; F. M. L. Thompson, 1988].

In order to clarify some of the questions about the relations between social classes it may be helpful to start with a simple analogy based on relationships at the individual level. Most of the possible relationships between two people would seem to fall into the following three broad categories: one person may choose to over-whelm the other by physical force, to manipulate the other by mental trickery, or to co-operate with the other through open agreement. In deciding which of these is taking place in any given case, it is important to set aside the question of motives, for physical force or mental manipulation may be chosen with the best of intentions, and open agreements may be entered into with an eye on personal gain. Thus, by analogy, the key issue in categorizing social relations should be, not the intentions of those involved but rather the behaviour they engage in. It is interesting to note that William Gladstone, emerging as a dynamic leader of the Liberal party in the 1860s on the basis of a campaign of popular speeches, thought in terms of precisely the three main options indicated above in defending his increasingly radical activities against aristocratic criticism from within his own party:

Please to recollect that we have got to govern millions of hard hands; that it must be done by force, fraud or goodwill; that the latter has been tried and is answering. [J. Morley, *The Life of William Ewart Gladstone. Volume II* (1903), p. 133. This quotation seems to have begun its now independent life in Perkin, 1969, *402*]

These distinctions of Gladstone's can be brought closer to current academic usage by labelling the three main forms of social relations coercion, control and consent, and this classification can then be made more comprehensive by adding the possibility of each one being stronger or weaker. This would then produce a spectrum of six possibilities for the relations between social classes running from the extreme of domination to the extreme of agreement, as laid out in Table 4.2.

Table 4.2 Six Possibilities for Social Relations

COERCION	Active repression
	Restriction of rights
CONTROL	Positive conditioning
	Exclusion of options
CONSENT	Passive acceptance
	Active participation

Clearly the strongest and most obvious form of physical coercion is active repression, above all by the armed forces, but this is normally only necessary when a widespread popular rebellion is actually taking place. Steps can be taken to prevent such a possibility by the less openly violent method of the restriction of rights to meet, communicate and organize opposition. This has the advantage of allowing rulers to deal with dissidents as individuals or small groups, and is often accompanied by the enforcement of public allegiance to the ruling ideology to make it easier to identify them. However, even in its weaker form this is still essentially a coercive method of rule and therefore one which does not guarantee long-term stability.

A more sophisticated and better established body of rulers may prefer to reduce physical coercion where possible and instead attempt to exercise control over people's minds. The most active

39

WOLVERHAMPTON POLYTECHNIC LIBRARY

form of this is positive conditioning into the desired set of values and norms, that is in effect brain-washing. A more liberal approach, which may be preferred because it gives people a greater sense of freedom, is to focus on the exclusion of undesirable options from their minds, but otherwise to leave them free to choose their own beliefs and behaviour. This is the most subtle method of domination as it is the one least likely to alert people (or outside observers) to the fact that they are being controlled, but it is also likely to be the most risky as it permits them a sense of real, if limited, freedom which may give them a taste and capacity for more.

However, it may not be felt necessary to exercise any kind of mental control at all for, if people show no serious inclination to challenge the power of their rulers, they may be left entirely to their own devices. This in turn may take two forms, both of which are equally genuine types of freedom. In the first place, people may simply passively accept their rulers without especially approving of them or of the way in which they govern. In the second place, they may feel a more positive agreement, at least over the basic framework of government, in which case they are more likely to participate actively within established institutions.

It might be objected that this clear distinction between six types of social relations is misleading, as societies are generally held together by a combination of a number of these possibilities and historians' work is bound to reflect this. Even if this is true, it should still be helpful to clarify which possibility is at issue at which moment, as well as to provide some guide to why certain combinations are more common than others, both in historical reality and in historical writing. Moreover, although some elements of coercion, control and consent will probably be found in all societies, it is also likely that one or another will be predominant in most cases. It is therefore now time to turn from these rather abstract considerations to examine the evidence for Britain in the second half of the nineteenth century, to see if it is possible to determine which of these possibilities was predominant in this case.

(ii) COERCION: REPRESSION AND RESTRICTION

The notion that British society in the second half of the nineteenth century was held together mainly by some form of coercion is the least plausible of the various possibilities and has not received wide support among historians. It is of course true that physical sanctions remained the basis of punishment for serious criminal offences and that the state was also prepared to remove the rights of some political extremists. However, these acts were directed at minorities on the margins of society and, compared to other European countries, Britain was notable for its low level of political and industrial violence after 1850. It had a remarkably small professional standing army; an unarmed and decentralized police force; notoriously inefficient intelligence services; and a continuing tradition of widening civil and political liberties which attracted both admiration and a constant stream of refugees from the rest of Europe.

If historians have therefore rarely argued that active repression was the basis of social order in Britain in the second half of the nineteenth century [though see Saville, 1987, and parts of Foster 1974], it is still worth considering this possibility in a little more detail, to clarify why it was not adopted by the ruling classes. In the first place, this can be understood in terms of the history of the state itself for, as an island nation, Britain needed not a strong army but a strong navy to defend itself against its external enemies: not only did this automatically weaken the state's coercive capacity in internal affairs, the British navy had a highly independent and insubordinate relationship with central government. Moreover, as a part of the heritage of resistance to absolutism in the seventeenth century, there remained a suspicion of centralization within the Establishment in general, with the Whigs going as far as to legitimize the subject's right of rebellion, and the British army itself being remarkably undisciplined and unhierarchical. Meanwhile, among the middle and lower classes libertarian attitudes were deeply rooted, particularly over such issues as resistance to military conscription, and the dislike of any separation of the armed forces from civilian life [Halévy, 1924]. Consequently, important sections of the ruling classes were acutely aware that repression only tended to stiffen protest, and they tried to avoid it as far as possible, even in situations which might seem most obviously to allow it [Bailey, 1981; Fox, 1985]. Thus in major industrial disputes in the late nineteenth and early twentieth centuries, even when troops were called in they were always subordinated to the civil authorities,

41

either local or national, who in turn had minimal statutory powers to enforce public order. Although there was a tendency towards increasing police powers and increasing centralization after 1900, this in itself led to a decrease in the use of the military, and was also accompanied by a long-term decline in violence during industrial disputes until the 1980s [Geary, 1985; Morgan, 1987].

The most frequent form of violent confrontation between the authorities and the people in modern Britain has therefore been what might be called the 'police riot', that is, a relatively non-violent crowd provoked as a result of being attacked by inexperienced and frightened law officers. The most notorious examples of this were Peterloo (1819), Newport (1839), and Glasgow (1919), with each case resulting in a great deal of public discussion and official self-justification, which tended retrospectively to exaggerate the threat of popular revolt [Stevenson, 1979; McLean, 1983].

Thus the relative absence of active repression in Britain after 1850 also has to be seen in the light of the absence of serious threats of popular revolt in the first place. This in turn can be linked to the absence of extensive restriction of rights, which allowed the working classes the space to deal with their most pressing problems within the framework of the existing legal system. Of course, the already mentioned weakness of repressive institutions would have undermined the enforcement of restriction, but in any case, following the defeat of absolutism in the seventeenth century, the British legal system had developed along lines which excluded the central state as far as possible: freedom from arbitrary detention (under Habeas Corpus), an independent judiciary, the jury system, and a high level of decentralization, all further weakened the possibility of extensive government restriction of rights. Indeed, since each of these particular guarantees of individual liberty was based on a strong underlying commitment to the rule of law in general, the British state can be seen as largely subordinate to society rather than vice versa [Halévy, 1924; Fox, 1985]. Moreover, the observable trend of legal and political rights in Britain in the nineteenth century was in a distinctly liberal direction, with increasing freedoms of speech and publication, of association and assembly, and with the opening up, especially after 1870, of Establishment institutions to participation by nonconformists of all kinds.

The most significant form of legal restriction in modern Britain

has therefore been emergency wartime legislation direct[
larly at the prevention of labour unrest, for example the Co...
tion Acts (1799–1824) and the Munitions of War Act (1915–19...
21). However, in the former case the legislation was primarily
intended as a weapon against political sedition and was therefore far
from fully enforced during ordinary industrial disputes, and in the
latter case the legislation was the outcome of a process of bargaining
between the government and the unions: in both cases the legal
restrictions were amended, and eventually repealed, in response to
trade union pressure [Brown, 1982; Fox, 1985; Reid, 1985]. Meanwhile, as has already been pointed out in Chapter 2 of this survey,
the overall trend of labour law and government policy on industrial
relations between 1850 and 1914 was broadly favourable to trade
unionism and free collective bargaining.

(iii) CONTROL: CONDITIONING AND EXCLUSION

Given the weakness of the repressive institutions and the widening
rights of citizens in modern Britain, if the social order was indeed
based on a form of domination it would have to have been a form of
mental control rather than physical coercion. This possibility has
attracted much more attention from historians, so much so that the
central project of British social history in the 1960s and 1970s can be
seen as an attempt to uncover and define the precise form of control
which was predominant in each period [E. P. Thompson, 1963;
Perkin, 1969].

The initial preference in the field was for an active and positive
conditioning of the population into a set of desirable moral values
and behavioural norms, such as hard work, punctuality, respect for
property and superiors, and so on: a process frequently referred to as
'social control'. This theory offered an attractive combination of
exposure of the mechanisms of power in an unequal society with an
explanation of why those without power had put up with their
position. It also provided an unusual opportunity for genuinely
inter-disciplinary co-operation between historians and sociologists,
including the participation of a number of internationally celebrated
critical theorists. Finally, and perhaps most importantly, it supplied
a unified guide to research in such diverse areas of cultural history as

43

family life, religion, leisure, education, crime and policing, social welfare, and the handling of deviant minorities [Donajgrodzki, 1977; Cohen and Scull, 1983]. Unfortunately, however, the growing body of detailed research in all of these fields has tended to undermine the usefulness of this approach for Britain after 1850.

In the first place, like the possibilities of coercion already considered, the idea that there was a need for positive conditioning of the population is often based on an exaggeration of the threat of popular revolt, particularly in the early years of the century. In fact most working people were generally disposed to be law-abiding, hard working, and 'respectable' given a reasonable minimum of justice and fair treatment [Brown, 1982]. Paradoxically, the notion of successful positive conditioning also tends to exaggerate the degree to which Britain after 1850 was a thoroughly orderly and peaceable society: while there may have been no serious threat of revolt there was still a higher level of disorder and conflict than would be fully consistent with the successful exercise of 'social control'. Despite the implications of some historical work, the analysis of relationships inside coercive institutions like prisons and mental asylums is of little use as a guide to social behaviour outside their walls, where choices were much wider and most people were inclined to exercise whatever independence they could in developing their own values and norms [Mayer, 1983]. Employers, for example, were still faced with skilled workers' job controls, absenteeism, and output lost through industrial disputes after 1850, and despite one or two attempts to argue the contrary, it is difficult to see either a skilled elite or trade unions as effective forms of employers' discipline [Foster, 1974; Price, 1980]. Not only were there occasional ugly episodes of violence during industrial disputes, as in Sheffield in the 1860s, the second half of the nineteenth century also saw incidents of public disorder during elections, unemployment demonstrations, and occasions of sectarian religious celebration. The overall level of violence may have been falling over the course of the century, but it is far from clear that this was due to the increasing effectiveness of control from above, and there was certainly no sharp break around 1850 [Stevenson, 1979; Bailey, 1981; F. M. L. Thompson, 1981].

Faced with these objections, proponents of the idea of successful positive conditioning are inclined to make their theory so flexible as to be untestable through empirical research. For example, it is sometimes implied that, simply because there was no popular revolt, there must have been an effective system of conditioning, and whatever the nature of popular values and activities they must therefore have been a result of ruling class control. This line of argument can even be taken as far as the claim that toleration of independent workers' organizations and occasional outbreaks of disorder was only a more subtle form of control through the creation of an illusory sense of freedom [Donajgrodski, 1977]. But when 'social control' is restricted to verifiable cases of attempted positive conditioning the theory rarely finds confirmation in the evidence for Britain after 1850.

While it is easy enough to find evidence of ruling-class disquiet over public order, or of middle-class 'moral entrepreneurs' determined to reform the masses, it is unsatisfactory to conclude from this that mechanisms of control were therefore established, let alone that they were effective [Stedman Jones, 1974; F. M. L. Thompson, 1981; Mayer, 1983]. For example, despite a great deal of activity on the part of pressure groups, there was not much success in areas like the prohibition of alcohol or the banning of fairs, partly indeed because of the reluctance of the police themselves to get involved in the enforcement which would have been necessary: even when prohibitive legislation was achieved, as in the case of off-course gambling, the local police frequently preferred to collude in widespread evasion [F. M. L. Thompson, 1981; Davies, 1991]. After all, if the industrial bourgeoisie was as socially and politically marginal as has been suggested in Chapter 2 of this survey, there is no reason to suppose that the state would have been particularly responsive to its demands for a disciplined workforce, especially if these cut against the prevailing tendency towards the liberalization of the legal system. There is indeed a growing body of evidence that there were important internal differences within the ruling classes in their attitudes towards popular behaviour, as significant as those over their own religious, political and cultural preferences [F. M. L. Thompson, 1988].

Even when 'moral entrepreneurs' did apparently get their way, for example in the establishment of new schools, of 'rational recreation', of working men's clubs, of new norms of female domestic behaviour, or of intrusive welfare provision, their aims were usually overwhelmed in the long run by the independence of popular attitudes.

Thus it seems that parents encouraged their children to attend schools in order to acquire literacy but not moral values, that football quickly threw off the mantle of Christian sportsmanship and became a livelier and more purely plebeian game, that working men's clubs not only abandoned their original temperance basis but also developed a new form of bawdy popular entertainment, that women continued to behave independently and to make full use of their opportunities outside the home, and finally that working-class communities retained their own norms of household management [Stedman Jones, 1974; Cunningham, 1980; F. M. L. Thompson, 1981; Johnson, 1985; Thane, 1988]. Indeed, it is precisely these areas which up to the present day have continued to provide the focus of concern for moral reformers keen to increase their control over the behaviour of others. Here, then, is another central paradox in the application of the positive conditioning approach to late nineteenth century Britain: it frequently relies on evidence of widespread complaints which are surely testimony to the autonomy of popular norms of behaviour, and thus to the strength of popular self-regulation in the sphere of socialization [Stedman Jones, 1974; Brown, 1982; Mayer, 1983; F. M. L. Thompson, 1988].

As a result, there has been a marked shift in more recent work away from the idea of positive conditioning. Many historians are, however, unwilling to abandon entirely the central assumption of a society held together by domination rather than agreement, and there has therefore been increasing interest in establishing a theory based on rulers' ability to exclude certain options from the minds of the people. Such an approach would clearly have many attractive features for late nineteenth century Britain, for it would play down the importance of physical coercion and allow for some real independence of popular attitudes. It would also be compatible with the revisionist view of the nature of the ruling classes outlined in Chapter 2 of this survey: all sections of the Establishment would have had an interest in maintaining their power and their property by excluding the possibility of revolt, even if they were unable to reach agreement on the content of positive conditioning.

This suggestion that there was a more subtle form of control has often been associated with the word 'hegemony' which has, however, also frequently been taken to cover almost every form of rule in unequal societies, from active repression to active participation

[Gray, 1977]. If it is to have any distinctive meaning, 'hegemony' ought perhaps to be more carefully reserved for the possibility of the exclusion of options. Moreover, considerably more attention ought to be paid to the mechanisms by which this might have occurred, for in much of the existing literature the emphasis is either on the general prevalence of ruling-class values, or on the relative freedom which sections of the working classes had to form their own ideas within such a framework [Gray, 1976; Tholfsen, 1976; Cunningham, 1980]. Since both of these emphases are also compatible with other forms of social relations, above all with forms of voluntary consent, they are not particularly helpful in advancing the specific concept of a more subtle form of control.

More recently this has been attempted through a focus on the way in which a series of historically-specific choices can create an institutional momentum, which in turn promotes a wide vested interest in existing procedures. The ruling classes may periodically consider other options but are likely to reject them because of the extra effort involved, and this makes it progressively more difficult for them to bring about a fundamental change of direction. While there is no simple conspiracy or direct attempt at control, the entrenched nature of existing institutions also tends to restrict popular perceptions, without implanting specific values or completely suppressing social conflict. For example, Alan Fox has argued that the British ruling classes gradually opted for a strategy of rule through a liberal industrial relations system, in which trade unions were recognized, bargaining was unrestrained by outside interference, and there were real gains for organized labour. As a result of the success of these arrangements, the possibility of the outright expropriation of private property was increasingly overshadowed in the minds of the working classes, without there being any form of positive conditioning into values which would have served the interests of industrial employers more directly [Fox, 1985]. Similarly, Ross McKibbin has argued that the ruling classes became increasingly committed to a constitutional system of political rule, in which the crown was seen as above politics, and parliament was seen as both representative of the people and bound to follow its own procedures. As a result of the relatively consistent application of these rules, the use of sporting metaphors became all-pervasive and unconstitutional activity began to seem intrinsically 'unfair', without there being much evidence of positive conditioning into values of deference or political submission [McKibbin, 1984].

However, although these emphases on an emerging preference for a particular strategy of rule and its apparent impact on popular political outlooks are indeed necessary parts of the idea of the exclusion of options, it is still not clear that they are sufficient to demonstrate that this, rather than voluntary consent, was indeed the prevailing form of social relations. And this is largely because these rather broad approaches are not entirely convincing in their identification of chronologically specific mechanisms by which particular limits were placed on the range of popular attitudes and ideas. After all, much the same legitimating ideology of liberty, justice and equity can be found in widely divergent periods of British history from at least as early as the thirteenth century.

Perhaps a more fruitful approach to the possibility of the exclusion of options might be developed along the lines indicated by Gareth Stedman Jones in his discussion of the appeal of Chartism in the late 1830s, and the movement's rapid collapse in the early 1840s. For the typical Chartist emphasis on the urgent need for an extended parliamentary franchise seems to have been significantly undermined by the Peel government's willingness to make major economic and social concessions within an as yet unreformed political system [Stedman Jones, 1983]. This historical approach therefore focuses on the way in which specific events affected the plausibility of particular political arguments. Moreover, by emphasizing the impact of the decisions of a prominent statesman, it also implies that the rather general notion of 'hegemony' might be grounded again in its original meaning of political leadership. Once a new strategic line of policy had begun to gain momentum, no doubt involving the orchestration of the mass media, the promotion of favourable cultural and intellectual spokesmen, an emerging parliamentary consensus, and perhaps even its eventual implantation into the education system, it is easy to appreciate how it could begin to overshadow other options and narrow the field of political vision.

One question remains, however: if the ability to exercise this kind of strategic leadership was dependent partly on making substantial responses to popular demands, can we be sure that it really remained a form of manipulation? In other words, historians who

48

are interested in developing this approach will need to establish a clear set of criteria to distinguish between covert domination and open bargaining in processes of political interaction.

(iv) CONSENT: ACCEPTANCE AND PARTICIPATION

There has, then, been a marked trend in social history during the 1980s away from its initial emphasis on a strong form of positive conditioning by the ruling classes and towards an increasing acknowledgement of the independence of working-class values and norms of behaviour. It may still be possible for historians to retain this within the framework of a theory of domination based on the ability of rulers to exclude certain options from the people's minds, and it seems likely that the next decade will be critical in determining whether such an approach really would be useful for Britain in the late nineteenth century. However, from the discussion of the other possibilities for social relations, it will already be apparent that there are a number of good reasons for taking seriously the idea that British society in this period might actually have been held together by some form of agreement or consent.

In the first place there is the elimination already indicated: there was neither a serious revolutionary threat nor evidence of extensive coercion; none of the attempts at positive conditioning seem to have worked very well; and it is still difficult to be precise about the mechanisms by which the ruling classes might have excluded options from their subjects' minds. Moreover, when historians apply these other approaches to Britain in this period they frequently begin by admitting the appearance of consent and then proceed to explain it away. It would therefore have the further attraction of greater simplicity to accept that social relations were, in fact, what they appeared to be. In this case both partners in the interaction would have been equally free to pursue their preferred goals and values: if the working classes did not pursue revolution it would have been because they genuinely did not want to, and if they agreed to the basic framework of society it would have been because they voluntarily chose to do so. This would still leave two possibilities of a more passive, apathetic consent, or 'acceptance', and a more active, positive consent, or 'participation'. In so far as consent has been

49

taken up by historians in recent years it has been largely along the lines of the former possibility, because this still allows for some hesitation before the acknowledgement that late Victorian society may indeed have been based on the positive approval of most of its members. Instead it emphasizes the economic and social conditions which pushed working people to accept the social order and created significant barriers which they would have to have overcome if they were to organize a successful rebellion.

Thus Gareth Stedman Jones has argued that by the mid-nineteenth century British capitalism had begun to appear more broadly and securely established, that it consequently became increasingly difficult to conceive of viable alternative arrangements, that, simply in order to live, working people therefore had to accept employment on the terms available, and that this in turn contributed towards the increasing stability of the system as a whole [Stedman Jones, 1975; see also F. M. L. Thompson, 1981]. In a more positive way, Kenneth Brown has argued that with the passage of time working people gradually came to accept an urban environment which was becoming more familiar, especially as many rural customs had been able to survive and new institutions of self-help were becoming increasingly effective [Brown, 1982]. Even more positively, a number of historians have emphasized the growing opportunities for employment and consumption in a period of unprecedented prosperity, which marked an absolute advance over the alternatives and was accepted by most working people as the best available, particularly because of the neutrality of the state implied by free trade and voluntary collective bargaining [McKibbin, 1984; Kirk, 1985; Benson, 1989].

At the more specific level of social relations within the workplace, it has been suggested that the process of de-skilling reduced workers' industrial and political independence, as employers took increasingly direct control over the mental parts of labour, especially after the introduction of automatic machinery [Stedman Jones, 1975; Joyce, 1980]. Although, as has been shown in the previous chapter, this now seems implausible as evidence mounts that skills remained high and employers' control over production processes remained loose, a similar point could be made in a more positive way by emphasizing how the survival of real skills and strong trade unions tended to fragment workers into distinct and sometimes even antagonistic sections, which it would have required a conscious effort to mobilize along the lines of a united working-class politics [Brown, 1982; Reid, 1983; McKibbin, 1984; Benson, 1989].

Outside the workplace attention has also been given to popular cultural pursuits from the point of view of passive acceptance, here again showing a range of more and less pessimistic emphases. Thus, at one end of the spectrum, Gareth Stedman Jones has argued that the vibrant radical culture of the early nineteenth century London artisans was undermined by an increasing separation between work and home and a retreat of popular pursuits into an increasingly inward-looking and fatalistic 'culture of consolation', above all in the pub and the music hall. Although impermeable to middle-class attempts at positive conditioning, this popular culture was spontaneously moving in a conservative direction, at least in the sense of becoming increasingly a-political [Stedman Jones, 1974; see also Cunningham, 1980]. With less emphasis on social alienation, Patrick Joyce has argued that the intimate involvement of Lancashire cotton employers in cultural provision within factory-based localities was effective in encouraging the spread of deferential attitudes as well as the entrenchment of marked pockets of specifically Conservative party loyalty. However, this was only because the employers, rather than attempting to reshape popular values, were careful to provide facilities which their workers genuinely enjoyed [Joyce, 1980]. Meanwhile, at the other end of the spectrum, Ross McKibbin has argued that the late nineteenth century saw the emergence of an increasing range of choice among cultural pursuits, many of which allowed the active development of intelligence, skill and organizational ability, in what might be called a genuine 'culture of satisfaction'. However, while in exceptional cases this may have provided a useful starting point for the careers of working-class Liberal and Labour leaders, its general effect was still to divide workers into separate clubs and associations and to divert popular energies away from politics [McKibbin, 1984]. Other important divisions in this area which have been increasingly highlighted include those by gender, generation, ethnic group and locality, all of which have certainly been under-emphasized in more simplistic notions of a homogeneous working-class culture [Reid, 1983; Johnson, 1985; Kirk, 1985; F. M. L. Thompson, 1988].

Finally, there is the arena of politics itself which has, perhaps not surprisingly, received less emphasis from social historians. It has, however, been suggested that poverty and the lack of available time and energy would have significantly weakened the political resources of the working classes, and that the narrowness of the effective franchise would have restricted their political power, at least as long as they were prepared to accept the limitations of constitutional methods [McKibbin, 1984; Benson, 1989]. Of course, these emphases on the lack of resources and opportunities would become less relevant as time went on and incomes rose, hours were reduced, trade unions and co-operative societies grew, the franchise was widened by further instalments of reform, and local party organizations ensured that more voters were registered and informed. While they may be more relevant for the earlier part of the period under consideration, they therefore seem less convincing as overall explanations of social order in Britain between 1850 and 1914 than the economic and cultural arguments for passive acceptance. *opposite lead to newst ae*

It would seem, then, that in so far as some form of consent has been advocated recently, it has been largely in terms of an emphasis on the working classes accepting their overall position in an unequal society in a relatively passive way. Although there has been an increasing interest in working people's ability to reshape their immediate environment in order to make it more tolerable, and consequently a tendency towards less pessimistic versions of passive acceptance, there still seems to be some unwillingness to acknowledge that British society after 1850 may have been held together by a more positive form of consent.

Perhaps this is because of a misunderstanding of what such a possibility would involve. For if it is defined in terms of total approval for the social order then it would clearly have no chance of survival as a serious option. However, in this form it is unlikely that it could apply to any social situation: even ruling classes are seldom in total agreement among themselves on every important issue. It would seem more reasonable, then, to define positive consent in terms of approval for the main institutions of public life and a willingness to participate within them whatever the actual goals being pursued: in other words, an agreement on how to disagree. One example of this kind of participation would be in industrial relations itself, for British employers were increasingly willing to recognize the rights of trade unions to organize, while the unions were generally willing to recognize the legitimacy of the private ownership of property. On everything else the two sides were likely to be in strong disagreement, but in principle were prepared to enter into bargaining over each other's goals. Given the absence of coercion and control, and given the active participation of the trade unions, this form of industrial relations would therefore have been based on positive consent, however severe the disputes which took place within it [Joyce, 1984; Reid, 1985]. It is interesting to note that, while such an approach was generally out of favour among historians in the 1960s and 1970s, like the newer emphases in the analysis of the nature of the major social classes, it too was more widespread before then [Halévy, 1924; though see also Best, 1971, and parts of Perkin, 1969].

One important area in which the idea of positive consent has been given more attention recently is in the discussion of the nature of the criminal law in modern Britain. As in social history more generally, most of the initial contributions tended to place the emphasis on domination, in terms of outright coercion, a strong form of control, or a combination of the two [Hay, 1975; Gatrell, 1980]. This is, after all, the area of public life in which physical sanctions are most prominent and the overt aim of the officials involved is clearly to reshape people's behaviour, but that should not in itself lead too quickly to assumptions about the wider social impact of law enforcement. Thus, as debates on the criminal law have continued and research has become more sophisticated, there has been a consistent trend towards the acknowledgement by historians of considerably more social equity and voluntary consent, as well as of unexpectedly high levels of active participation on the part not only of the middle classes but also of the lower classes. This discussion has so far been most fruitful for the eighteenth century [Innes and Styles, 1986], but that in itself is of some significance, as a growth of popular confidence in the way in which the law is administered will normally be an important precondition for the emergence of more active participation in other areas of social and political life. That such popular approval was indeed maintained as a central element in nineteenth century law enforcement has been shown by recent research on the operation of local magistrates' courts, which were able to offer informal arbitration in the case of local quarrels, and financial relief for individual cases of hardship, as well as prosecution for common criminal offences like theft and assault. Even the poorest working people were prepared to make use of all of these facilities, including prosecution, in large part because the magistrates were sensitive to popular ways of life and definitions of justice [Davis, 1984].

At this point it may be tempting to argue that such participation on the part of the working classes was purely instrumental, reflecting no particular approval of the social order. It is therefore important to remember the general point that it is not motive but behaviour which defines the nature of the relations between social groups: the possibility of self-interest would not weaken the observation of active participation, and of course the satisfaction of self-interest is likely to be a significant element in the emergence of subjective approval. In any case it is also important to remember that active participation does not imply total approval even of the institutions involved, only a willingness to take part in them, which may indeed be partly motivated by a desire to change the way they function in order to improve their benefits for particular groups.

If the eighteenth century was a crucial period in the extension of this kind of participation within the legal system, the nineteenth century was a crucial period in its extension within electoral politics. Even before the successive enlargements of the parliamentary franchise in 1832, 1867, 1884, and 1918, Britain had possessed significantly representative political institutions which were subject to more or less effective popular pressure through rioting, public meetings, petitions and an uncensored press [Halévy, 1924]. Moreover, one group which was still notoriously excluded from the widening franchise in the late nineteenth century was nevertheless able to increase its political participation: women were becoming highly active as canvassers and fund raisers within party electoral machines, above all through the Primrose League (1883), the Women's Liberal Federation (1886), and the Women's Labour League (1906) [Hollis, 1987; Thane, 1988]. Indeed they even managed to gain the vote in local elections in boroughs in 1869, and to consolidate their rights of membership of local school and poor law boards in the early 1870s, so that by the 1900s women provided respectively over 500 and over 1000 of the representatives on these bodies in England and Wales [Hollis, 1987, *486*]. It seems likely

54

that similar patterns of participation would also have been found among men still excluded from the widening franchise, especially after the abolition of the property qualification for local office in 1878, and the creation of more representative local government at the county and parish level in 1888 and 1894 respectively.

This marked growth in popular political participation during the nineteenth century was also dependent on an increasing sense that, despite its distance from the problems of everyday life, party politics might sometimes offer genuine remedies. This has already been touched on in the previous section in discussing the contribution of Peel's concessions to the collapse of Chartism in the 1840s [see also Mandler, 1990, for Whig concessions in the 1840s], and the same point has been made in a more positive way in H. C. G. Matthew's account of the contribution of Gladstone's tax reforms to the building of a 'mid-Victorian social contract' in the 1850s and 1860s. The minimizing of protective tariffs on imports made government seem more impartial; the strict review of spending, above all on defence, made government seem less corrupt; and the switch of the burden of taxation away from consumption and towards income and wealth made government seem more popular. Moreover, Gladstone saw all of these rather technical matters as issues of supreme public importance, built strong links with the trade unions and the national and provincial press, and pioneered the appearance of executive politicians at mass meetings throughout the country [Matthew, 1986; see also Biagini and Reid, 1991]. Both the content of these reforms and the style of their presentation intensified the process by which party politics was coming to be seen as increasingly relevant to the problems of everyday life, further encouraging the active participation in local and national elections which was gradually becoming available to wider sections of the population.

Of course, this did not lead to an exclusive affiliation to Gladstonian Liberalism and a good deal of recent research has been concerned with the strength of popular Conservatism: in assessing the subjective attitudes of those who participated in elections, it is therefore necessary to distinguish between two main forms of positive consent. On the one hand there was that more usually connected with the idea of consent in political theory, consisting of a commitment to the rights of all citizens to individual freedom and increasingly equal participation in public life, alongside a belief in the possibility of

55

progressive improvements in all aspects of society. This would normally have attached working-class voters to the Liberal party in the second half of the nineteenth century, and was often accompanied by a rather austere emphasis on self-improvement, and by Nonconformist religious affiliations [Tholfsen, 1976]. On the other con hand there was that connected more with an acceptance of inequality, consisting of a willingness to defer to the existing hierarchical order, and emphasizing the dangers of attempting to change anything which already seemed to work well enough. This would normally have attached working-class voters to the Conservative party in the second half of the nineteenth century, and was often accompanied by a greater emphasis on sociability and enjoyment, and by Anglican religious affiliations [Joyce, 1980]. It is important to recognize that both 'citizenship' and 'deference' were equally voluntary and therefore equally conditional on the satisfaction of the participants' perceived self-interest. Despite its close connection with the acceptance of inequality, 'deference' was just as much a form of positive consent, its maintenance was just as dependent on the delivery of anticipated benefits by the more powerful partner in the implicit social contract, and its expression in popular politics could be just as assertive and independent.

This, of course, also implies that there was no widespread support for state socialism, whether of a revolutionary or a reformist type, among British working people in this period. If from the point of view of passive acceptance this would be attributed to the strength of capitalism and the absence of viable socialist alternatives, from the point of view of active participation it would be attributed to a positive popular preference for a largely liberal and self-regulating society. Thus there would be no paradox involved in acknowledging the existence of widespread hostility to increases in government regulation and intrusion, alongside a long-term trend towards positive consent. It would simply be that in this period the public life the working classes approved of was one in which it was still expected that the activities of the central state would be kept within clear limits [Pelling, 1968b; Thane, 1984; Biagini and Reid, 1991].

In assessing the application of the main forms of social relations to Britain between 1850 and 1914, it therefore seems that coercion through active repression or the restriction of rights would be the least appropriate of the possibilities. Moreover, control through positive conditioning has become increasingly vulnerable in the face of a growing body of research, and its more subtle version of the exclusion of options still needs to be made historically specific. Currently, then, it would appear that the strongest candidate for the predominant form of social relations in Britain after 1850 is consent, both through the passive acceptance of economic and social conditions, and through increasingly active participation in the legal and political systems.

It is worth pointing out once again that consent as defined in this survey is not intended to imply either enthusiastic approval for every aspect of existing conditions or equality in the distribution of power. On the contrary, passive acceptance may result from a deeply-rooted fatalism or from the difficulty of organizing alternatives. Even in the case of active participation, the agreement would only be over how to disagree, it might well be accompanied by demands for immediate material benefits or for long-term improvements in the functioning of established institutions, and such demands in turn might be rejected by those with more power. However, as long as it is possible for citizens to organize to assert their demands free from coercion or control, and as long as the response to those demands is an open one, it can safely be concluded that they do indeed live in a society based on consent.

Those who are still unconvinced might consider the contrast between the experience of Britain and her major European neighbours in this period. Indeed a more systematic programme of comparative study would be very valuable, not only to clarify the nature of the predominant social relations in each case, but also to open up the question of the historical interaction between these relations and the classes involved in them. In the case of Britain for example, it might be asked how far consent emerged as the predominant form of rule because of the persistence of aristocratic leadership among the ruling classes, in combination with a continued reliance on working classes with high levels of skill and independence. Or perhaps these characteristics of the main social groups were made possible by a national preference for managing social interaction through bargaining and compromise.

Further research on local and national politics, on popular recourse to the law, and on other opportunities for participation by different groups will no doubt clarify whether the passive or the active form of consent was becoming more important in late nineteenth century Britain, and what weight should be assigned to the 'citizenship' and 'deference' versions of the latter. But in the meantime it may be worth making some rough guesses about these questions through a consideration of the national electoral statistics in Table 4.3.

Table 4.3   Electorate, Turn-out, and Conservative and Liberal Votes, 1852–1910

	a Electorate 000s	b Turn-out as % of a	c Conservative as % of b	d Liberal/Labour as % of b
1852	1185	58	41	58
1857	1236	59	33	65
1859	1272	64	34	66
1865	1350	63	40	60
1868	2485	69	38	62
1874	2753	66	44	53
1880	3040	72	42	55
1885	5708	81	44	47
1886	5708	74	51	45
1892	6161	77	47	45
1895	6331	78	49	46
1900	6731	75	50	46
1906	7265	83	43	54
1910	7695	87	47	51
1910	7710	82	47	50

Source: F. W. S. Craig, *British Electoral Facts 1832–1987* (1989). Tables 4.01, 7.01, 7.02, 7.05.

These figures would suggest that active participation was growing in importance throughout the period: not only was the franchise being extended, there was also a trend towards an increased turn-out at elections of those entitled to vote, partly as a result of the increasing number of contested constituencies. Paradoxically, as more citizens were able to exercise political rights, their positive commitment to the values of liberalism seems to have declined, from the unmatched predominance of Gladstone in the late 1850s and 1860s to a position of more equal competition between Liberals and

Conservatives in the 1890s and 1900s. Perhaps this can be understood in terms of a widespread sense of the need for major reforms in the mid-nineteenth century, followed by a growing sense of satisfaction at all levels of society about the progress that had been made towards a fairer and more participatory system of government. Or perhaps the influence ran altogether the other way, and it was the increasingly close electoral competition between the major parties which made it seem worthwhile making the individual effort to vote.

The theory of consent thus turns out to have perhaps unexpected potential for the measurement of change and for the suggestion of lines of causal inquiry. For, since it is still often associated with the naïve 'whig' belief in the inevitability of progress which was widespread in the nineteenth century, it is often assumed that there is something fundamentally a-historical about it. On the contrary, it may be the theories of coercion and control which are less sensitive to historical change: for their focus tends to be on the containment of isolated incidents of revolt at widely separated moments of time; on the construction of relatively monolithic systems of restriction and conditioning which either function or break down; and on the resolution of political crises in such a way as to secure the strategic control of the dominant classes. Thus, in addition to a rather static quality, these approaches share a heavy emphasis on the activities of the ruling classes and tend to portray the working classes as more or less passive objects of successful systems of rule. On the other hand, an emphasis on consent not only requires closer attention to popular attitudes but may also be better able to measure their change over time, in terms of patterns both of consistent growth and of swings and reversals. If it really is the case that all three forms of social relations are always present in some degree, perhaps the real loss in understanding comes when the element of consent is overlooked even within societies which are held together predominantly by coercion and control.

5 Conclusions

One common theme which has run through the preceding discussions of the ruling classes, the working classes and social relations in Britain between 1850 and 1914 has been the observation of the completion of an intellectual cycle. With the increasing influence of social science on history in the 1960s, a new emphasis was placed on the rise to power of the bourgeoisie, the increasing subordination of the industrial working class, and the maintenance of domination by a strong form of control. However, as each of these issues has been pursued in more detail, there has been a marked return during the 1980s to the previous historical emphasis on the persistence of aristocratic power, the increasing independence of the working classes, and the centrality of voluntary agreement in a social order based on consent. To some extent the departures of the 1960s can be understood in terms of social history's need to justify its expansion by having something distinctive to say, but it seems likely that this intellectual cycle has also been the result of a cycle in contemporary public life more generally, of over-optimism about the possibility of fundamental changes in society, followed by frustration, and then by a reassessment of the value of existing traditions.

A second theme common to all three areas of discussion has been the inadequacy of simple horizontal divisions, above all that into capital against labour, and an emphasis instead on the importance of vertical divisions within both the ruling classes and the working classes: between branches of economic activity, between regions, and between religious and political affiliations. Enough studies have now been done to make it worth summarizing in Table 5.1 the interplay of these influences on four types of popular identity which have recurred in this survey, bearing in mind that this is not intended as a comprehensive picture of British society in the period.

The first main point which is highlighted by this table is the importance of diversity in social conditions. Perhaps a society held

60

Table 5.1   Four Types of Popular Identity

	Anglican	Nonconformist
Craft sectors	Fatalistic Conservative: London East End	Libertarian Liberal: Glasgow metal working
Seniority sectors	Paternalistic Conservative: Lancashire cotton	Statist Liberal: North East coalfields

together by coercion or control would become more homogeneous under pressure from above, but one held together mainly by consent is likely to contain a variety of popular identities. The second main point which is highlighted is the independent impact of ideas and values in shaping these identities: although economic interest played an important part it did not of itself determine either denominational or party affiliations. For both these reasons it is therefore time to stop looking for a single concept to open up all the secrets of nineteenth century society, and instead to focus on building up a more systematic framework for the comparison of the interaction between economic, cultural and political influences in different parts of the country.

Despite, or perhaps indeed because of, their omission, this table also acts as a reminder of the persistent lag in studies of the British ruling classes. A great deal more still has to be done to clarify the range of employers' attitudes towards labour in different industries, the relationships between employers and other major groups in the local propertied classes, the impact of elite politics on popular politics in each area, and the balance of forces influencing the adoption of specific policies at the national level. The frequent recurrence of the professional middle classes throughout this survey suggests that more research could usefully be done on this group in particular, especially in the closing decades of the nineteenth and the early decades of the twentieth century, when it was becoming increasingly important in both local and national politics.

Another theme which has recurred in this survey, and which this time is included in the table, is the important role of religion in the shaping of popular identities. Although this has been suggestively explored in some studies, particularly of Lancashire Conservatism, religion has still to receive the full weight it deserves as the central

61

element in cultural life for most members of British society in the second half of the nineteenth century. This is one area where work on the ruling classes is currently more advanced than that on the working classes for, while the doctrinal background to elite politics has recently received increasing attention from historians, the understanding of the impact of different religious denominations on popular ideas, beliefs and forms of organization is still at a very rudimentary level. One important issue which seems likely to have been closely connected with denominational differences is the question of popular attitudes towards the state, particularly over matters concerning the legitimate use of power and the scope for local democracy. It would therefore be very useful to have more research on the different attitudes and forms of association to be found in popular religious and political life in different parts of the country.

Here it will also be important to bear in mind different experiences of existing power relations and, from the discussion in Chapter 3, it would seem likely that occupational experiences were particularly important. It can indeed be suggested that groups of workers would more often have moved horizontally across the table between forms of Conservatism and forms of Liberalism, and increasingly after 1914 forms of support for the Labour party, than that they would have moved vertically from an attitude appropriate for their type of skill and self-organization to one more appropriate for a different occupational experience (though this is by no means impossible). Thus while religious traditions and the effectiveness of political appeals would have been the major determinants of which party was supported, occupational experiences are likely to have remained a basic influence on which current of policy was supported within that party.

The contribution of detailed local studies to the understanding of nineteenth century society is therefore far from exhausted, though, given the emphasis on the diversity of conditions, it can no longer be expected that any one such study will provide a direct explanation for major developments in national politics. Instead, it will be important simultaneously to build up a more sophisticated picture of change at the national level, and a number of points which have been raised in this survey have suggested that it may be useful to see this in broadly cyclical terms. In terms of party politics, for example, it will be remembered from Table 4.3 that the Liberal predominance in the 1850s and 1860s was replaced by a marked swing towards Conservatism in the 1870s and particularly the 1880s, and that this in turn was succeeded by a major Liberal revival in the 1900s. Similarly, it has been noted that the peaks of trade union influence on government policy were in the 1860s and early 1870s, when the Second Reform Act and union legal immunities were achieved; and again in the 1900s, when the Board of Trade was active in promoting collective bargaining, and the unions established independent parliamentary representation through the Labour party. Outbursts of bitter popular protest on the other hand seem to fit this cycle inversely: with Chartism emerging in the 1830s and collapsing in the early 1840s, to be replaced by a more constitutional radicalism in the 1850s and 1860s; while the discontent expressed in the unemployment marches and the New Unionism of the 1880s was increasingly integrated within the parliamentary progressive alliance of the 1900s.

These trends would seem to give initial confirmation to the idea of cycles in public life, of roughly twenty years of sharp contraction and roughly thirty years of broad expansion, along the following lines: a period of contraction from 1825–42, followed by expansion from 1843–74, then another period of contraction 1875–88, followed again by expansion 1889–1921, and so on. Each period of contraction would have been characterized by relative economic depression; a decline in popular self-organization, measured particularly in terms of trade union strength; a general swing at all levels of society towards more conservative, restrictive and centralized policies; less scope for popular participation in public life; and an increase in social and political conflict. Conversely, each period of expansion would have been characterized by relative economic prosperity; a growth in trade union strength; a general swing towards more liberal, expansionist and decentralized policies; increasing popular participation; and a stronger sense of social and political consensus.

Adopting such a cyclical perspective would then lead to significantly different assessments of symbolic moments of popular protest which have been widely taken as marking major turning points in the study of nineteenth century society. Chartism, for example, would be seen, not as the climax of a long crisis of early industrialization in need of containment by a special new stabilization of capitalism, but rather as the product of a combination of economic,

63

social, and political factors specific to the contraction phase 1825–42, and likely to be replaced by greater political integration and participation during the next phase of expansion. Similarly, the 'revival of socialism' in the 1880s would be seen not as the long overdue conclusion to a unique mid-century period of stabilization and the beginning of the properly modern class struggle, but rather once again as the specific product of the contraction phase 1875–88, with the subsequent period of expansion, including the formation of the Labour party itself, having more in common with the heyday of mid-Victorian Liberalism than has generally been appreciated.

A good deal more research and discussion would obviously be needed to establish whether this really is a useful way of periodizing modern British history, and how exactly the various elements in such broad cycles might have interacted. But whether it turns out to be useful or not, the brief description of this approach should have made it clear that developing a sophisticated picture of national developments will require close co-operation between historians working in previously separate time periods, as well as between specialists in economic, social and political history. If this sort of co-operation can be increased, alongside the more systematic regional comparison of popular identities, then the study of nineteenth century British society will indeed have come of age.

Select Bibliography

Bailey, V. (ed.) (1981). *Policing and Punishment in Nineteenth Century Britain.* Eight essays highlighting the particular, frequently local, contexts of changes in coercion.

Benson, J. (1989). *The Working Class in Britain, 1850–1939.* An important survey, emphasizing passive acceptance and the differences between large-scale and more traditional industry.

Best, G. (1971). *Mid-Victorian Britain, 1851–70.* A lively introduction, suggesting the importance of economic prosperity and working-class 'deference'.

Biagini, E. F. (1987). 'British Trade Unions and Popular Political Economy 1860–1880', *Historical Journal,* 30. A challenging reinterpretation, stressing the effective use trade unionists made of liberal economic theory.

Biagini, E. F. and Reid, A. J. (eds) (1991). *Currents of Radicalism. Popular Radicalism, Organized Labour and Party Politics in Britain, 1850–1914.* Eleven essays highlighting the continuities in popular support for radical liberalism.

Brown, K. D. (1982). *The English Labour Movement, 1700–1951.* An important survey, emphasizing rising standards of living, widespread moderation and sectional divisions.

Cannadine, D. (1980). *Lords and Landlords: The Aristocracy and the Towns 1774–1967.* Highlights the persistence of aristocratic involvement, in Birmingham and Eastbourne.

Cannadine, D. (1984). 'The Present and the Past in the English Industrial Revolution, 1880–1980', *Past and Present,* 103. A stimulating account of changing interpretations in economic history.

Cohen, S. and Scull, A. (eds) (1983). *Social Control and the State. Historical and Comparative Essays.* Thirteen essays by historians and sociologists, mainly on crime and insanity, and generally critical of control.

Cole. G. D. H. (1937). 'Some Notes on British Trade Unionism in the Third Quarter of the Nineteenth Century', *International Review of Social History*, 2 (1937), reprinted in E. M. Carus-Wilson (ed.), *Essays in Economic History. Volume 3* (1962). A pioneering comparison of craft and seniority forms of organization.

Cole, G. D. H. (1952). *Introduction to Economic History, 1750–1950*. A popular introduction, suggesting the importance of themes which have been rediscovered in the 1980s.

Cole, G. D. H. (1955). *Studies in Class Structure*. A challenging criticism of Marxism, stressing rising standards of living, new industrial skills, and the survival of small-scale property.

Coleman, D. C. (1973). 'Gentlemen and Players', *Economic History Review*, 26. A stimulating discussion of the persistent influence of gentlemanly values on British businessmen.

Crafts, N. F. R. (1985). *British Economic Growth During the Industrial Revolution*. An important survey of the quantitative evidence for the gradualist view of economic growth.

Cunningham, H. (1980). *Leisure in the Industrial Revolution, c. 1780–c. 1880*. An important survey, emphasizing the survival of autonomous popular culture, contained by 'hegemony'.

Davidson, R. (1978). 'The Board of Trade and Industrial Relations, 1896–1914', *Historical Journal*, 21. Argues that the government strengthened moderate trade unionism and consensual industrial relations as a means of control.

Davies, A. (1991). 'The Police and the People: Gambling in Salford, 1900–1939', *Historical Journal*, 34. A pioneering oral study, suggesting the ineffectiveness of policing and the influence of poverty in shaping autonomous popular values.

Davis, J. (1984). 'A Poor Man's System of Justice: the London Police Courts in the Second Half of the Nineteenth Century', *Historical Journal*, 27. A challenging revisionist account of law enforcement, stressing popular consent.

Donajgrodzki, A. P. (ed.) (1977). *Social Control in Nineteenth Century Britain*. Nine essays applying the concept to crime, education, religion, leisure and social policy, with a useful introduction by the editor.

Foster, J. (1974). *Class Struggle and the Industrial Revolution. Early Industrial Capitalism in Three English Towns*. A controversial study of the Lancashire cotton town of Oldham, arguing that a revolutionary working class was contained by increasing bourgeois unity and social control through a supervisory labour aristocracy. [See Stedman Jones, 1975; Joyce, 1980; and Kirk, 1985.]

Fox, A. (1985). *History and Heritage. The Social Origins of the British Industrial Relations System.* An important survey, emphasizing the deep roots of liberalism, and arguing that it was a subtle form of control.

Garrard, J. (1983). *Leadership and Power in Victorian Industrial Towns 1830–80.* Shows both the reality of manufacturers' power and its limits, in Bolton, Rochdale and Salford.

Gash, N. (1965). *Reaction and Reconstruction in English Politics, 1832–1852.* Stimulating reflections on the limits of reform and the persistence of aristocratic government.

Gatrell, V. A. C. (1980). 'The Decline of Theft and Violence in Victorian and Edwardian England', in V. A. C. Gatrell, B. Lenman and G. Parker (eds), *Crime and the Law. The Social History of Crime in Western Europe since 1500.* A major argument for the enforcement of the criminal law as a form of control.

Gatrell, V. A. C. (1982). 'Incorporation and the Pursuit of Liberal Hegemony in Manchester, 1790–1839', in D. Fraser (ed.), *Municipal Reform and the Industrial City.* Highlights the lower middle-class basis of Manchester liberalism.

Geary, R. (1985). *Policing Industrial Disputes: 1893–1985.* Highlights the long-term decline in violence.

Grampp, W. D. (1960). *The Manchester School of Economics.* Highlights the radical political ideals of the Anti-Corn Law League leaders.

Gray, R. (1976). *The Labour Aristocracy in Victorian Edinburgh.* Adapts the theory [see Hobsbawm, 1954] to take account of the large numbers of low-paid skilled workers, and the independent values of organized labour.

Gray, R. (1977). 'Bourgeois Hegemony in Victorian Britain', in J. Bloomfield (ed.), *Class, Hegemony, and Party.* Critical of 'social control', but uses 'hegemony' to cover all forms of rule.

Gray, R. (1981). *The Aristocracy of Labour in Nineteenth-Century Britain, c. 1850–1914.* A critical survey, emphasizing the diversity of experiences and the need for a wider explanation of social stability.

Green, E. H. H. (1988). 'Rentiers versus Producers? The Political Economy of the Bimetallic Controversy, *c.* 1880–1898', *English Historical Review*, 103. Highlights the greater commitment of financiers to free trade, and the political weakness of manufacturers.

Gunn, S. (1988). 'The "Failure" of the Victorian Middle Class: a Critique', in Wolff and Seed [1988]. Critical of Rubinstein [1981a] and Wiener [1981]; argues for increased unity of all propertied groups around a commitment to the free market.

Guttsman, W. G. (1963). *The British Political Elite.* Contains valuable quantitative evidence on the persistence of aristocratic political power up to 1914.

Halévy, E. (1924). *A History of the English People in 1815.* The first volume of a classic survey, emphasizing the weakness of the central state and the importance of religion in creating consent.

Harrison, R. (ed.) (1978). *The Independent Collier: The Coal Miner as Archetypal Proletarian Reconsidered.* Eight essays, focusing on miners' struggles for independence and the diversity of local conditions.

Harrison, R. and Zeitlin, J. (eds) (1985). *Divisions of Labour. Skilled Workers and Technological Change in Nineteenth Century England.* Six essays analysing the impact of craft unions on the division of labour.

Hay, D. (1975). 'Property, Authority and the Criminal Law', in D. Hay *et al.*, *Albion's Fatal Tree. Crime and Society in Eighteenth Century England.* An influential essay, arguing for the enforcement of the criminal law as a means of ruling-class control.

Hennock, E. P. (1973). *Fit and Proper Persons. Ideal and Reality in Nineteenth Century Urban Government.* Highlights party conflict and the importance of retailers and professionals, in Birmingham and Leeds.

Hobsbawm, E. J. (1949). 'Trends in the British Labour Movement since 1850', *Science and Society*, 13 (1949), revised and reprinted in Hobsbawm [1964]. An influential article, arguing for the containment of revolution through the economic gains available to trade unionists: first a labour aristocracy then the working class as a whole.

Hobsbawm, E. J. (1954). 'The Labour Aristocracy in Nineteenth-century Britain', in J. Saville (ed.), *Democracy and the Labour Movement, Essays in Honour of Dona Torr*, reprinted in Hobsbawm [1964]. Develops Hobsbawm [1949] through a detailed study of wage differentials. See Gray [1976] and Pelling [1968a].

Hobsbawm, E. J. (1964). *Labouring Men. Studies in the History of Labour*. An influential collection of essays covering a wide range of topics in nineteenth century labour history.

Hollis, P. (1987). *Ladies Elect. Women in English Local Government, 1865–1914*. A pioneering survey, emphasizing women's active participation in politics.

Hopkins, E. (1975). 'Small Town Aristocrats of Labour and their Standard of Living, 1840–1914', *Economic History Review*, 28. Highlights the differences between industries and the impact of unemployment, in Stourbridge.

Howe, A. (1984). *The Cotton Masters, 1830–1860*. Contains useful evidence, which rather undermines the author's own conclusion that the factory owners were a coherent and assertive group.

Howkins, A. (1985). *Poor Labouring Men. Rural Radicalism in Norfolk, 1870–1923*. A pioneering study of agricultural trade unionism, highlighting the local and religious roots of radicalism.

Innes, J. and Styles, J. (1986). 'The Crime Wave: Recent Writing on Crime and Criminal Justice in Eighteenth-Century England', *Journal of British Studies*, 25. Criticizes Hay [1975] and stresses the importance of active participation.

Johnson, P. (1985). *Saving and Spending. The Working Class Economy in Britain, 1870–1939*. Highlights the distinctiveness of working-class saving patterns, and their contribution to a diversity of popular life-styles.

Joyce, P. (1980). *Work, Society and Politics. The Culture of the Factory in Later Victorian England*. An important study of the Lancashire cotton towns, emphasizing the economic and cultural dependence of workers on their employers, and the strength of popular Conservatism. See Kirk [1985].

Joyce, P. (1984). 'Labour, Capital and Compromise: a Response to Richard Price', *Social History*, 9. Highlights the common interests in the employment relationship.

Kirk, N. (1985). *The Growth of Working Class Reformism in Mid-Victorian England*. Critical of Foster [1974] and Joyce [1980]; highlights rising incomes and improved workers' organization, alongside increasing ethnic divisions.

Kitson Clark, G. (1962). *The Making of Victorian England*. A classic survey of politics in its social context, emphasizing the persistence of the aristocracy and the importance of religion.

Lazonick, W. H. (1979). 'Industrial Relations and Technical Change: The Case of the Self-Acting Mule', *Cambridge Journal of Economics*, 3. An important case study, stressing employers' preferences for self-regulating groups of workers and the influence of trade unions over the work process.

Mandler, P. (1990). *Aristocratic Government in the Age of Reform. Whigs and Liberals 1830–1852*. Highlights aristocratic willingness to concede to popular pressure.

Matsumura, T. (1983). *The Labour Aristocracy Revisited. The Victorian Flint Glass Makers, 1850–80*. Contains valuable evidence on a seniority sector, despite its rather misleading title.

Matthew, H. C. G. (1986). *Gladstone, 1809–1874*. An important reassessment, placing the politician in a wide intellectual and social context.

Mayer, J. A. (1983). 'Notes towards a Working Definition of Social Control in Historical Analysis', in Cohen and Scull [1983]. A critical survey of the application of the concept in American social history.

McClelland, K. and Reid, A. J. (1985). 'Wood, Iron and Steel: Technology, Labour and Trade Union Organization in the Shipbuilding Industry, 1840–1914', in Harrison and Zeitlin [1985]. Analyses of one of the strongest cases of craft union control over the work process.

McKendrick, N. (1986). '"Gentlemen and Players" Revisited: the Gentlemanly Ideal, the Business Ideal and the Professional Ideal in English Literary Culture', in N. McKendrick and R. B. Outhwaite (eds), *Business Life and Public Policy. Essays in Honour of D. C. Coleman*. An important survey, emphasizing the subordination of business values to gentlemanly and professional values.

McKibbin, R. (1984). 'Why Was There No Marxism in Great Britain?', *English Historical Review*, 99, reprinted in R. McKibbin, *The Ideologies of Class. Social Relations in Britain, 1880–1950* (1990). A stimulating essay, suggesting the importance of passive acceptance and the influence of established political institutions.

McLean, I. (1983). *The Legend of Red Clydeside*. A challenging revision of the myth of a revolutionary labour movement in this region.

Melling, J. (1980). ' "Noncomissioned Officers": British Employers and their Supervisory Workers, 1880–1920', *Social History*, 5. A pioneering study of foremen in engineering and shipbuilding, suggesting ambiguities in their position.

More, C. (1980). *Skill and the English Working Class. 1870–1914.* An important survey of methods of training, emphasizing high levels of real skill throughout the economy.

Morgan, J. (1987). *Conflict and Order. The Police and Labour Disputes in England and Wales, 1900–1939.* Highlights the decline of local democratic control of policing in the twentieth century.

Morris, R. J. (1990). *Class, Sect and Party. The Making of the British Middle Class, Leeds 1820–1850.* Highlights the importance of party and religious divisions within the middle class, as well as the predominance of commercial and professional groups.

Pelling, H. (1967). *Social Geography of British Elections, 1885–1910.* An encyclopaedic guide to local electoral behaviour in its social context. See also Tanner [1990].

Pelling, H. (1986a). 'The Concept of the Labour Aristocracy', in Pelling [1986b]. The classic criticism of the concept, including valuable insights on skills, incomes, working-class organization, and politics.

Pelling, H. (1968b). *Popular Politics and Society in Late Victorian Britain.* An important collection of essays, stressing widespread moderation and dislike of state interference.

Perkin, H. (1969). *The Origins of Modern English Society, 1780–1880.* An influential survey, arguing for the imposition of entrepreneurial values on nineteenth century society, mainly through control but with elements of consent.

Perkin, H. (1989). *The Rise of Professional Society. England Since 1880.* A stimulating survey, focusing on the rise of professional values from the late nineteenth century.

Prest, J. (1990). *Liberty and Locality. Parliament, Permissive Legislation, and Ratepayers' Democracies in the Nineteenth Century.* Highlights the growth of general permissive acts, and their requirement of local democracy.

Price, R. (1980). *Masters, Unions, and Men. Work Control in Building and the Rise of Labour 1830–1914.* Argues for revolutionary potential in workers' resistance to de-skilling, contained by the moderation of trade union officials.

71

Price, S. (1981). 'Riveters' earnings in Clyde shipbuilding, 1889–1913', in *Scottish Economic and Social History*, 1. Contains valuable evidence on low earnings among skilled workers, due to unemployment and lower piece rates.

Reid, A. J. (1983). 'Intelligent Artisans and Aristocrats of Labour: the Essays of Thomas Wright', in J. Winter (ed.), *The Working Class in Modern British History. Essays in Honour of Henry Pelling.* Argues for the contribution of individual choices and generational shifts to differences within the working classes.

Reid, A. J. (1985). 'Dilution, Trade Unionism and the State in Britain During the First World War', in S. Tolliday and J. Zeitlin (eds), *Shop Floor Bargaining and the State. Historical and Comparative Perspectives.* Highlights the centrality of skilled labour in wartime, and the state's need to win its consent.

Roberts, E. (1984). *A Woman's Place. An Oral History of Working-Class Women, 1890–1940.* A pioneering oral study of North Lancashire, with stimulating insights into all aspects of working-class life.

Roberts, E. (1988). *Women's Work, 1840–1940.* A valuable introduction to the complexities of female participation in paid labour.

Rubinstein, W. D. (1981a). *Men of Property. The Very Wealthy in Britain since the Industrial Revolution.* An important quantitative study of wealth-holding, demonstrating the relatively low standing of manufacturers.

Rubinstein, W. D. (1981b). 'New Men of Wealth and the Purchase of Land in Nineteenth-century Britain', *Past and Present*, 92, reprinted in W. D. Rubinstein, *Elites and the Wealthy in Modern British History* (1987). Argues that few businessmen bought landed estates, and that the aristocracy was a closed caste.

Samuel, R. (1977). 'The Workshop of the World: Steampower and Hand Technology in Mid-Victorian Britain', *History Workshop*, 3. An encyclopaedic survey of work methods, emphasizing the central contribution of human inputs.

Saville, J. (1987). *1848. The British State and the Chartist Movement.* Argues for the centrality of active repression in maintaining social order.

Smith, D. (1982). *Conflict and Compromise. Class Formation in English Society, 1830–1914.* Highlights patterns of division within the middle classes, in Birmingham and Sheffield.

Smith, J. (1984). 'Labour Tradition in Glasgow and Liverpool', *History Workshop*, 17. Suggests the importance for labour politics of differences between Liberal and Conservative traditions.

Stedman Jones, G. (1974). 'Working-Class Culture and Working-Class Politics in London, 1870–1900; Notes on the Remaking of a Working Class', *Journal of Social History*, 7, reprinted in Stedman Jones [1983]. An important criticism of 'social control', stressing the emergence of a spontaneously a-political working-class culture.

Stedman Jones, G. (1975). 'Class Struggle and the Industrial Revolution', *New Left Review*, 90, reprinted in Stedman Jones [1983]. An influential criticism of Foster [1974], arguing for passive acceptance due to increased economic stability and widespread de-skilling.

Stedman Jones, G. (1983). 'Rethinking Chartism', in Stedman Jones [1983]. An important analysis of the rise and fall of Chartism in primarily political terms.

Stedman Jones, G. (1983). *Languages of Class. Studies in English Working Class History, 1832–1982*. An influential collection of essays, combining social theory and historical research.

Stevenson, J. (1979). *Popular Disturbances in England, 1700–1870*. Highlights the role of broad economic and social change in reducing disorderly behaviour.

Stone, L. and Stone, J. C. F. (1984). *An Open Elite? England 1540–1880*. Argues that few businessmen bought landed estates, but notes the cultural and political openness of the aristocracy.

Tanner, D. M. (1990). *Political Change and the Labour Party, 1900–18*. An important survey of local experiences, emphasizing different currents within parties, appealing to different occupational groups.

Tebbutt, M. (1983). *Making Ends Meet. Pawnbroking and Working-Class Credit*. Contains valuable evidence on working-class budgeting and life-styles.

Thane, P. (1984). 'The Working Class and State "Welfare" in Britain, 1880–1914', *Historical Journal* 27. A challenging essay, stressing popular preferences for independence and self-government.

Thane, P. (1988). 'Late Victorian Women', in T. R. Gourvish and A. O'Day (eds), *Later Victorian Britain, 1867–1900*. A stimulating survey, emphasizing areas of growing women's independence.

73

Tholfsen, T. R. (1976). *Working Class Radicalism in Mid-Victorian England*. Argues for the 'hegemony' of liberalism over radicalism, on the basis of a prior underlying consensus.

Thompson, E. P. (1963). *The Making of the English Working Class*. An influential argument for a revolutionary threat in the early nineteenth century, based on skilled workers' resistance to de-skilling and government repression, contained by increasingly united ruling class control.

Thompson, F. M. L. (1963). *English Landed Society in the Nineteenth Century*. The classic study of the landed classes, stressing the slow decline of aristocratic power.

Thompson, F. M. L. (1977). 'Britain', in D. Spring (ed.), *European Landed Elites in the Nineteenth Century*. Focuses on the success of the 'aristocratic embrace' between 1880 and 1914.

Thompson, F. M. L. (1981). 'Social Control in Victorian Britain', *Economic History Review, 34*. An important survey, critical of the concept and suggesting the importance of consent.

Thompson, F. M. L. (1988). *The Rise of Respectable Society. A Social History of Victorian Britain, 1830–1900*. Highlights diversity and continuity in social conditions.

Trainor, R. (1985). 'Urban Elites in Victorian Britain', *Urban History Yearbook*. Argues for the influence of the middle classes in industrial regions based on their growing wealth and unity.

Wiener, M. (1981). *English Culture and the Decline of the Industrial Spirit, 1850–1980*. Controversial for its claim that an increase in the influence of aristocratic values after 1850 explains Britain's economic decline. See McKendrick [1986] and Gunn [1988].

Williams, R. (1958). *Culture and Society 1780–1950*. An influential survey of the social values of English literary culture, arguing that it was slow to accept industry and democracy.

Wolff, J. and Seed, J. (eds) (1988). *The Culture of Capital: Art, Power and the Nineteenth Century Middle Class*. Seven pioneering essays on provincial middle-class culture.

Wood, S. (ed.) (1982). *The Degradation of Work? Skill, Deskilling and the Labour Process*. Nine essays by historians and sociologists challenging simplistic ideas about de-skilling.

Young, G. M. (1936). *Portrait of An Age. Victorian England*. A classic account of the impact of competing political traditions on the formation of the state, and the generational shifts in patterns of ideas.

Zeitlin, J. (1985). 'Engineers and Compositors: a Comparison', in Harrison and Zeitlin [1985]. An important comparative study, stressing the influence on the work process of the relative effectiveness of workers' and employers' organizations.

Index

Labour party, 32, 34, 35, 36, 51, 54, 62, 63, 64
Lancashire
  factory owners, 15, 18, 20, 51, *see also* factory reform
  local politics, 20
  popular politics, 35, 51, 61
landowners, 10–11, 13, 14–15, 16, 18, 20, 22, 37
law
  criminal, 53–4
  liberal nature of British, 23, 41, 42–3, 45
  see also labour law
Lazonick, W. H., 27–8
liberalism, 20, 22, 23–4, 55–6, 58–9, *see also* free trade, law, political economy
Liberal party, 34, 35, 36, 51, 54, 55–6, 58–9, 61, 62–3
literary culture, 21
local government, 17, 19–20, 54–5
London
  popular politics, 51, 61
  wealth-holding, 15

machinery, 27–30, 50
Marx, K., 25–6
Matthew, H. C. G., 55
McKendrick, N., 21
McKibbin, R., 47, 51
merchants, 14, 15, 17, 20, 22
metal working, 28, 34, 61
Methodists, 35
middle classes, 12–13
  culture, 22–3, 41, 45–6
  see also bankers, farmers, industrialists, merchants, professions, retailers, ruling classes
monarchy, 17, 23

Nonconformists, 56, 61
north east of England, popular politics, 61

Oxbridge, 17, 21–2

Peel, R., 48, 55
Pelling, H., 32
Perkin, H., 9
police force, 41–2, 45
political economy, 22–3
political parties, 22, 23, 35, 52, 54–6, 58–9, 61–4, *see also* Conservative, Labour, Liberal
popular politics, *see* Glasgow, Lancashire, London, north east of England
professions, 17, 18, 20, 21–2, 61
public schools, 17, 21–2

regional identities, 60–2
religion, 22, 23, 35, 61–2, *see also* Anglicans, Evangelicalism, Methodists, Nonconformists
retailers, 20, 22
riots, 42, 44, 54
Rubinstein, W. D., 14–15
ruling classes, 9, 10–11, 19, 24, 41, 45, 46, 47, 52, 61, 62, *see also* aristocracy, landowners, middle classes

Smith, A., 22
social control, 11, 30, 43–5, 53
socialism, 56, 64
social relations, 38–40, 56–9, *see also* citizenship, deference, hegemony, social control
Stedman Jones, G., 48, 50, 51
strikes, 41–2, 43, 44

tax reform, 55
Thompson, E. P., 9
Thompson, F. M. L., 16
trade unions, 19, 23, 27–8, 29, 30, 32, 34–5, 43, 44, 47, 50, 52, 53, 55, 63, *see also* employers' strategies, labour law, strikes

wages and incomes, 31–2, 33, 50, 52
women
  employment, 33

77